HARCOURT HORIZONS
★★★★★★★★★★★★

States and Regions

Activity Book

Harcourt

Orlando   Austin   Chicago   New York   Toronto   London   San Diego

Visit *The Learning Site!*
www.harcourtschool.com

The activities in this book reinforce social studies concepts and skills in **Harcourt Horizons: States and Regions.** There is one activity for every lesson and skill in the Pupil Edition. Copies of the activity pages appear with answers in the Teacher's Edition. In addition to activities, this book also contains reproductions of the graphic organizers that appear in the chapter reviews in the Pupil Edition. Multiple-choice test preparation pages for student practice are also provided. A blank multiple-choice answer sheet can be found after these content pages.

Contents

Name _____   Date _____

Multiple-Choice
Answer Sheet

Number your answers to match the questions on the test preparation page.

____	Ⓐ Ⓑ Ⓒ Ⓓ	____	Ⓐ Ⓑ Ⓒ Ⓓ	____ Ⓐ Ⓑ Ⓒ Ⓓ
____	Ⓕ Ⓖ Ⓗ Ⓙ	____	Ⓕ Ⓖ Ⓗ Ⓙ	____ Ⓕ Ⓖ Ⓗ Ⓙ
____	Ⓐ Ⓑ Ⓒ Ⓓ	____	Ⓐ Ⓑ Ⓒ Ⓓ	____ Ⓐ Ⓑ Ⓒ Ⓓ
____	Ⓕ Ⓖ Ⓗ Ⓙ	____	Ⓕ Ⓖ Ⓗ Ⓙ	____ Ⓕ Ⓖ Ⓗ Ⓙ
____	Ⓐ Ⓑ Ⓒ Ⓓ	____	Ⓐ Ⓑ Ⓒ Ⓓ	____ Ⓐ Ⓑ Ⓒ Ⓓ

____	Ⓐ Ⓑ Ⓒ Ⓓ	____	Ⓐ Ⓑ Ⓒ Ⓓ	____ Ⓐ Ⓑ Ⓒ Ⓓ
____	Ⓕ Ⓖ Ⓗ Ⓙ	____	Ⓕ Ⓖ Ⓗ Ⓙ	____ Ⓕ Ⓖ Ⓗ Ⓙ
____	Ⓐ Ⓑ Ⓒ Ⓓ	____	Ⓐ Ⓑ Ⓒ Ⓓ	____ Ⓐ Ⓑ Ⓒ Ⓓ
____	Ⓕ Ⓖ Ⓗ Ⓙ	____	Ⓕ Ⓖ Ⓗ Ⓙ	____ Ⓕ Ⓖ Ⓗ Ⓙ
____	Ⓐ Ⓑ Ⓒ Ⓓ	____	Ⓐ Ⓑ Ⓒ Ⓓ	____ Ⓐ Ⓑ Ⓒ Ⓓ

____	Ⓐ Ⓑ Ⓒ Ⓓ	____	Ⓐ Ⓑ Ⓒ Ⓓ	____ Ⓐ Ⓑ Ⓒ Ⓓ
____	Ⓕ Ⓖ Ⓗ Ⓙ	____	Ⓕ Ⓖ Ⓗ Ⓙ	____ Ⓕ Ⓖ Ⓗ Ⓙ
____	Ⓐ Ⓑ Ⓒ Ⓓ	____	Ⓐ Ⓑ Ⓒ Ⓓ	____ Ⓐ Ⓑ Ⓒ Ⓓ
____	Ⓕ Ⓖ Ⓗ Ⓙ	____	Ⓕ Ⓖ Ⓗ Ⓙ	____ Ⓕ Ⓖ Ⓗ Ⓙ
____	Ⓐ Ⓑ Ⓒ Ⓓ	____	Ⓐ Ⓑ Ⓒ Ⓓ	____ Ⓐ Ⓑ Ⓒ Ⓓ

____	Ⓐ Ⓑ Ⓒ Ⓓ	____	Ⓐ Ⓑ Ⓒ Ⓓ	____ Ⓐ Ⓑ Ⓒ Ⓓ
____	Ⓕ Ⓖ Ⓗ Ⓙ	____	Ⓕ Ⓖ Ⓗ Ⓙ	____ Ⓕ Ⓖ Ⓗ Ⓙ
____	Ⓐ Ⓑ Ⓒ Ⓓ	____	Ⓐ Ⓑ Ⓒ Ⓓ	____ Ⓐ Ⓑ Ⓒ Ⓓ
____	Ⓕ Ⓖ Ⓗ Ⓙ	____	Ⓕ Ⓖ Ⓗ Ⓙ	____ Ⓕ Ⓖ Ⓗ Ⓙ
____	Ⓐ Ⓑ Ⓒ Ⓓ	____	Ⓐ Ⓑ Ⓒ Ⓓ	____ Ⓐ Ⓑ Ⓒ Ⓓ

____	Ⓐ Ⓑ Ⓒ Ⓓ	____ Ⓐ Ⓑ Ⓒ Ⓓ
____	Ⓕ Ⓖ Ⓗ Ⓙ	____ Ⓕ Ⓖ Ⓗ Ⓙ
____	Ⓐ Ⓑ Ⓒ Ⓓ	____ Ⓐ Ⓑ Ⓒ Ⓓ
____	Ⓕ Ⓖ Ⓗ Ⓙ	____ Ⓕ Ⓖ Ⓗ Ⓙ
____	Ⓐ Ⓑ Ⓒ Ⓓ	____ Ⓐ Ⓑ Ⓒ Ⓓ

© Harcourt

Name _____ Date _____

MAP AND GLOBE SKILLS
Read a Map

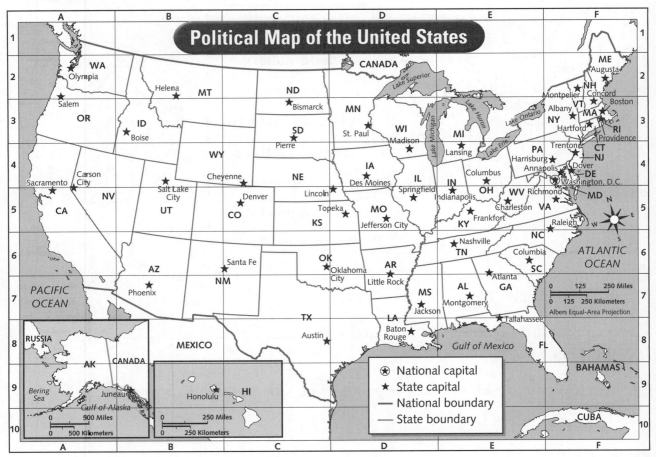

Directions **Use the map of the United States to answer these questions.**

1 What does a star surrounded by a circle represent on the map? _____

2 What two inset maps are part of this map? Why do you think those areas are

shown in inset maps? _____

_____

3 What city is located in square B–3? _____

4 In which direction would you travel to go from Nebraska to Texas? _____

5 About how many miles is it from Salem, Oregon, to Madison, Wisconsin?

_____

Why Geography Matters

Directions Use the terms in the box below to complete the sentences.

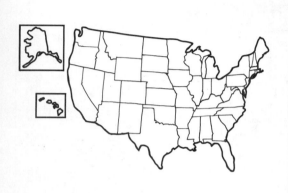

| geography |
| geographers |
| location |
| physical features |
| human features |
| interact |
| region |

1 Formed by nature, _____ include landforms, bodies of water, and plant life.

2 Because humans and their surroundings _____, they affect one another.

3 When you study Earth and the people who live on it, you are studying

_____.

4 Buildings, roads, and cities are all examples of _____.

5 A _____ is an area on Earth whose features make it different from other areas.

6 Every place on Earth has its own space, or _____.

7 _____ do much more than find places on maps. They learn all they can about places and the people who live there.

Why History Matters

Directions Below are some homework assignments for a history class. Use the tasks listed in the box to identify the purpose of each assignment. Write the task in the space provided. You will use one of the tasks twice.

Learning About Time	Identifying Points of View
Finding Evidence	Drawing Conclusions

1 Read the letters in your textbook written by a woman who owned slaves during the Civil War. Then read the diary entries in your textbook written by one of her slaves who learned to read and write after she escaped to freedom. Use these two sources to understand the different ways people of that time period felt

about their lives. _____

2 While you read Chapter 4 of your textbook, make a list of the major events that occurred before the American Revolution. Compare those events, and think about how they affected one another. Then analyze all the information together

to decide why the American Revolution happened. _____

3 Interview your grandparents or other family members about when your family first came to the United States. Ask to see old photographs, paintings, letters, birth certificates, or journals belonging to your family. Use all of these sources to write a report on the history of your family in the United States.

_____

4 Do research at the library or on the Internet to find when the first settlers arrived in your state, when your state joined the United States, when your state capital was chosen, and other important events in your state's history. Then display the information in a time line titled "The History of My State."

_____

5 Do research at the library or on the Internet to find speeches given by the people who ran for President of the United States in the last election. Use these sources to understand the different opinions each person had on important issues at the

time. _____

Name _____   Date _____

Compare Primary and Secondary Sources

Directions Decide whether each of the items below is a primary or secondary source. Write *P* for a primary source or *S* for a secondary source in the space provided. Then under each item, explain your answer.

1 _____ the United States Constitution

_____

2 _____ a history textbook written today about an event that took place in 1861

_____

3 _____ a newspaper story written about a hurricane, based on the author's interviews of people who saw the storm

_____

4 _____ the transcript of a speech given by the President of the United States

_____

5 _____ a soldier's diary describing a battle in which the soldier took part

_____

6 _____ a photograph of a crime scene

_____

7 _____ an encyclopedia article about the building of the pyramids

_____

8 _____ a videotape recording of a baseball game

_____

Why Economics Matters

Directions Use the clues to complete the word puzzle. The shaded line of letters will show you the theme of the puzzle.

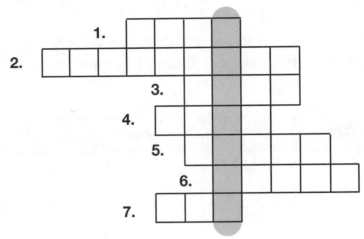

Clues

① Most people _____ money to pay for college in the future.

② An economy is the way people use _____ to meet their needs.

③ Hospitals, schools, farms, and factories are just a few of the many places where people _____.

④ A _____ is a place where people keep their money.

⑤ People make, buy, sell, and trade _____ to meet their needs.

⑥ Most people have jobs or own businesses in order to make _____.

⑦ If you do not live and work on a farm, you probably _____ most of the food you eat.

Why Civics and Government Matter

The United States government passes laws to help people live together peacefully and safely. Many of these laws describe the important rights and responsibilities you have as a citizen of the United States.

Directions Each right shown in the chart below is guaranteed by law in the United States. Complete the chart by describing why you think each right is important.

RIGHT	WHY IS IT IMPORTANT?
Freedom of speech	_____ _____ _____
Freedom of religion	_____ _____ _____
Freedom to write and publish	_____ _____ _____
The right to gather with other citizens	_____ _____ _____
The right to ask the government for action or help in solving problems	_____ _____ _____

© Harcourt

Use after reading Introduction, page 9.

Name ______________________ Date ______________

Why Culture and Society Matter

Directions Interview your family members to learn about your family's cultural heritage. Then complete the chart below.

MY CULTURAL HERITAGE

My family name: ______________________

Where my early family members came from: ______________________

____

Languages my early family members spoke and languages my family speaks today: ______________________

____

Holidays my family celebrates: ______________________

____

____

Special ways of doing things that are part of my family's cultural heritage:

____

____

____

Special foods that are part of my family's cultural heritage:

____

____

____

Use after reading Introduction, page 10.

Where on Earth Is the United States?

Directions Complete the following activities to describe where the United States is on Earth.

1 In which hemispheres is the United States located?

_____

2 Use oceans and continents to describe the global address of the United States.

_____

_____

3 Describe the relative location of the United States, using its relation to other countries.

_____

_____

_____

4 Use bodies of water to describe the relative location of the United States.

_____

_____

_____

5 Describe the location of your state in relation to other states in the United States.

_____

_____

_____

_____

© Harcourt

Name _____   Date _____

MAP AND GLOBE SKILLS

Use Latitude and Longitude

The years between 1492 and 1522 are often called the Great Age of Exploration. During those years many European nations sent ships and explorers to look for new lands and riches. In fact, by the end of the Great Age of Exploration, Europeans had sailed all the way around the world!

Directions **Use the map below to answer the questions on page 10.**

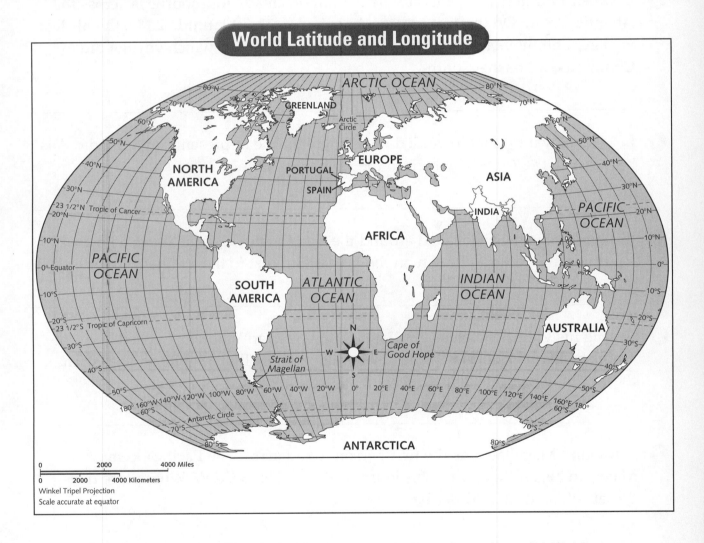

World Latitude and Longitude

(continued)

1 Between 1492 and 1522, most explorers set sail from two European countries that lie at latitude 40°N. Which countries are these?

_____

2 In 1488 Bartholomeu Dias sailed as far south as 35°S, 20°E before returning home to Europe. Dias reached the tip of what continent?

_____

3 Between 1492 and 1502, Christopher Columbus made four journeys across the Atlantic Ocean. On the first voyage, he sailed to about latitude 20°N. On his last voyage, Columbus reached a latitude of about 10°N. On which voyage did Columbus sail farther south?

_____

4 In 1497 Giovanni Caboto landed near 50°N latitude in present-day Canada. Was he closer to the Arctic Circle or to the Antarctic Circle?

_____

5 In 1498 Vasco da Gama sailed around the tip of Africa to India. Which lines of longitude and latitude shown on the map are closest to the southern tip of India?

_____

6 During his voyage between 1501 and 1502, Amerigo Vespucci crossed both the Tropic of Cancer and the Tropic of Capricorn. What line of latitude does each of these named parallels represent?

_____

7 Ferdinand Magellan was the first person to sail across the Pacific Ocean. Magellan began that part of his journey at about 55°S, 70°W. What place does this absolute location describe?

_____

Name _____ Date _____

The Land

As early explorers, settlers, and visitors traveled throughout North America, they often described the land they saw. In many cases, their descriptions provided the first glimpses of the great variety of landforms in the United States.

Directions From the list below of landforms in the United States, choose one to match each of the descriptions that follow. In the space next to each quotation, write the name of the landform that the person described.

Appalachian Mountains	**Grand Canyon**
Central Valley	**Great Basin**
Coastal Plain	**Great Plains**
Columbia Plateau	**Rocky Mountains**

1 _____ "A level, blasted region . . . Far as one could see . . . there was nothing but desert."
_____ —British traveler Isabella Lucy Bird, 1873

2 _____ "Our landing place . . . is mostly level; the soil is sand and earth. All throughout it there are very large trees."
_____ —Spanish explorer Álvar Núñez Cabeza de Vaca, 1542

3 _____ "Making your way through the mazes of the Coast Ranges . . . lies the great . . . valley glowing golden in the sunshine . . . one smooth, flowery, lake-like bed of fertile soil."
—American naturalist John Muir, 1868

4 _____ "Mountains . . . running nearly parallel with the sea-coast . . . of the Atlantic."
_____ —United States leader Thomas Jefferson, 1781

5 _____ "I reached some plains, so vast that I did not find their limit anywhere that I went . . . there was not a stone, nor a bit of rising ground, nor a tree, nor a shrub."
_____ —Spanish explorer Francisco Vásquez de Coronado, 1541

6 _____ "Vast mountains of rock eternally covered with snow."
—American explorer William Clark, 1805
_____

MAP AND GLOBE SKILLS

Read an Elevation Map

Directions Study this elevation map, and read each sentence below. Circle *T* if the sentence is true and *F* if it is false. If the sentence is false, cross out the word that makes it false and write above it the correct word to make it true.

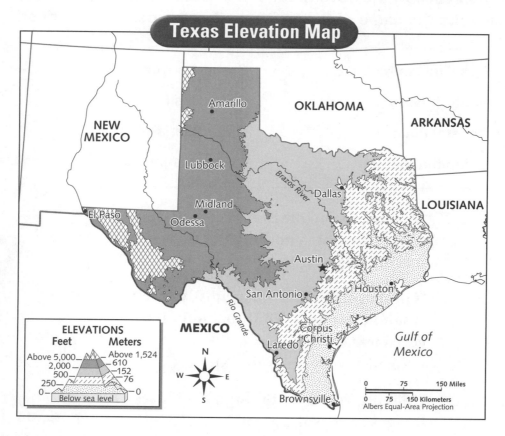

1. Lubbock has a higher elevation than Corpus Christi.　　　　T　　　F

2. The highest parts of Texas are located in the south.　　　　T　　　F

3. Most of Texas lies below sea level.　　　　T　　　F

4. Brownsville has a lower elevation than Austin.　　　　T　　　F

5. None of the land along the Texas–New Mexico border is higher than 2,000 feet above sea level.　　　　T　　　F

6. Austin and San Antonio are located in the same range of elevations.　　　　T　　　F

Looking at Rivers

Directions Use the map of Major Rivers of the United States on page 40 of your textbook to complete the following sentences.

1 The _____ River flows across the entire state of Alaska.

2 The Mississippi River begins in the state of

_____ and empties into the _____ .

3 The _____ River forms most of the border between Vermont and New Hampshire.

4 The Platte River is a tributary of the _____ River.

5 The Alabama River empties into the Gulf of Mexico near

the city of _____ .

6 A river called the _____ forms much of the border between the United States and Mexico.

7 Five cities located along the Mississippi River are

_____ , _____ , _____ ,

_____ , and _____ .

8 From Montana, the Missouri River flows east into

the state of _____ .

9 The city of Chicago is located on the

_____ River.

10 The Columbia River flows mostly through the state

of _____ .

Use after reading Chapter 1, Lesson 3, pages 38–43.

Climate Across the United States

Because the United States is so large, it includes nearly every kind of climate known on Earth. In order to study and compare different climates, people often divide the world into climate regions. The areas within each region share similar average temperatures and precipitation levels.

Directions The chart on page 15 describes six main categories of climate on Earth. The map below it shows where these climate regions occur across the United States. Use the chart and map to answer the following questions.

1 What is the only state in the United States that has areas with a polar climate?

Why do you think this kind of climate is found there? _____

_____

2 Which states have areas with a tropical climate? How do those states' locations

explain why they have this kind of climate? _____

_____

_____

_____

3 What landform causes parts of the United States to have a highland climate?

_____

4 In what parts of the United States are most of the desert or semiarid climates

located? _____

5 What are the main differences between a temperate warm climate and a
temperate cold climate? How does location help explain these differences?

_____

_____

_____

(continued)

Use after reading Chapter 1, Lesson 4, pages 44–48.

REGION	CLIMATE
Tropical	Temperatures are usually very hot year-round. It can be rainy all year or have two seasons—one wet and one dry.
Desert or Semiarid	It is dry year-round or has only a short rainy season. Temperatures can be either hot or cold.
Temperate Warm	Rain falls throughout the year but is heaviest during the long summers. Summer temperatures are usually hot, and winters are short and mild.
Temperate Cold	Winters can be long, cold, and snowy. Summers are short but may be very hot.
Highland	High elevations bring cool or cold temperatures year-round.
Polar	Temperatures are very cold most of the year.

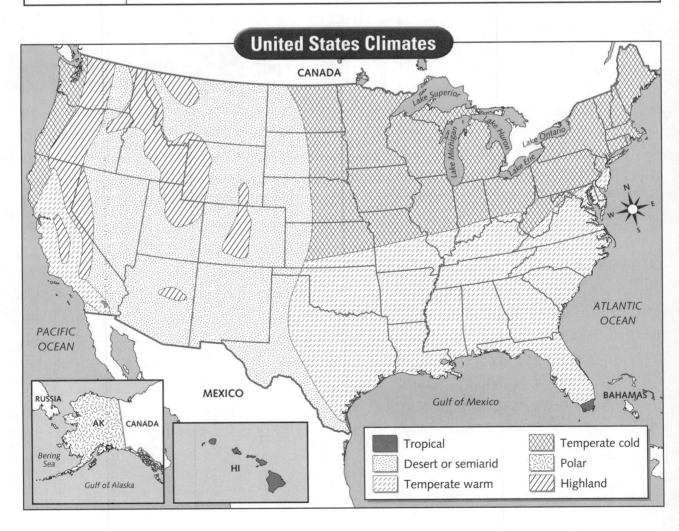

United States Climates

Legend:
- Tropical
- Desert or semiarid
- Temperate warm
- Temperate cold
- Polar
- Highland

© Harcourt

Name _____ Date _____

Natural Resources

Many of the products that people use every day are made from natural resources. Because natural resources are limited, conservation is very important. Waste from the products people use creates large amounts of garbage—about 230 million tons a year in the United States alone. By understanding this and limiting what we throw away, we can reduce the amount of garbage produced. This will help conserve resources and protect the environment.

Directions **Use the bar graph to answer these questions.**

1 What material makes up the largest part of the garbage produced in the United States each year?

_____

2 About how much glass do people in the United States throw away each year?

_____

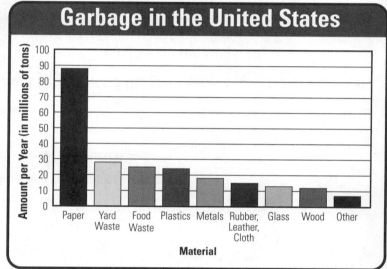

3 Each year, people recycle about half of all the yard waste produced in the United States. About how much yard waste do Americans

recycle each year? _____

4 What are some ways you and your family could cut down on the amount of

garbage you throw away each day? _____

_____

_____

_____

_____

Use after reading Chapter 1, Lesson 5, pages 49–53.

Name _____ Date _____

CHART AND GRAPH SKILLS
Use Tables to Group Information

In addition to preserving resources in national forests, the United States government also sets aside large areas of the country to preserve as national parks.

Directions Read the information in Table A about national parks in the United States. Classify that same information in Table B by size, from largest park to smallest park. Then use both tables to answer the questions that follow.

Table A: United States National Parks, in Alphabetical Order		
NATIONAL PARK	**LOCATION**	**ACRES**
Acadia	Maine	41,933
Badlands	South Dakota	242,756
Grand Canyon	Arizona	1,217,158
Great Smoky Mountains	North Carolina and Tennessee	520,269
Olympic	Washington	922,651
Yosemite	California	761,236

Table B: United States National Parks, in Order by Size		
ACRES	**LOCATION**	**NATIONAL PARK**

1 In which state is Olympic National Park located? In which table was it easier to find this information? _____

2 Which park listed in the tables is the largest? In which table was it easier to find this information? _____

3 Where is Great Smoky Mountains National Park? Which table did you use to find this information? Explain why you used that table. _____

_____

4 In what other ways could you classify this information about national parks in tables? _____

_____

© Harcourt

Our Country's Geography

Directions Use this graphic organizer to show that you understand how the chapter's main ideas are connected. Complete it by writing two details about each main idea.

There are many ways to describe locations in the United States.

1._____

_____

_____

2._____

_____

People use natural resources.

1._____

_____

_____

2._____

_____

_____

The United States has many landforms.

1._____

_____

2._____

_____

Resources

Location

Landforms

Our Country's Geography

Climate

Rivers

The climate varies across the United States for several reasons.

1._____

_____

2._____

_____

Rivers both wear down and build up the land.

1._____

_____

2._____

_____

© Harcourt

Use after reading Chapter 1, pages 20–55.

Name _____ Date _____

Test Preparation

Directions Read each question and choose the best answer. Then fill in the circle for the answer you have chosen. Be sure to fill in the circle completely.

1 The United States is located on the continent of—
- Ⓐ Europe.
- Ⓑ South America.
- Ⓒ Asia.
- Ⓓ North America.

2 What mountains run along most of the Pacific Coast of the United States?
- Ⓕ Appalachian Mountains
- Ⓖ Rocky Mountains
- Ⓗ Sierra Nevada
- Ⓙ Coast Ranges

3 The place where a river empties into a larger body of water is called the river's—
- Ⓐ mouth.
- Ⓑ source.
- Ⓒ channel.
- Ⓓ floodplain.

4 Which of the following is *not* a factor that affects a place's weather?
- Ⓕ the precipitation
- Ⓖ the wind
- Ⓗ the economy
- Ⓙ the temperature

5 It is important to conserve fuels because those resources are—
- Ⓐ nonrenewable.
- Ⓑ expensive.
- Ⓒ renewable.
- Ⓓ polluted.

Regions Around You

Directions Fill in the lines of the box below to describe where you live.
Then in the diagram that follows, color your state on the map of the United
States. In the state box, name your state. Then fill in the other boxes of the
diagram to name the regions where you live.

WHERE I LIVE

NAME _____

STREET ADDRESS _____

CITY OR TOWN _____

STATE _____

REGION _____

COUNTRY _____

CONTINENT _____

HEMISPHERES _____

Regions Within Regions

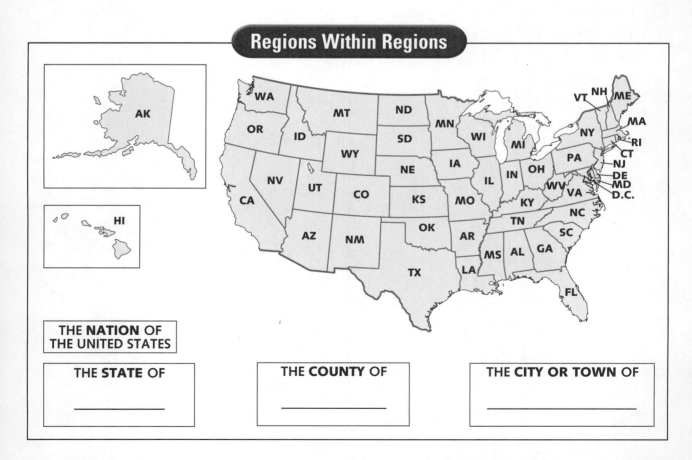

THE **NATION** OF
THE UNITED STATES

THE **STATE** OF
_____

THE **COUNTY** OF
_____

THE **CITY OR TOWN** OF
_____

Use after reading Chapter 2, Lesson 1, pages 60–64.

© Harcourt

Other Kinds of Regions

Directions Use the clues to fill in the words from 1 to 7. When you have finished, read the letters inside the shaded boxes from top to bottom to see the theme of this puzzle. A black box means a space between two words.

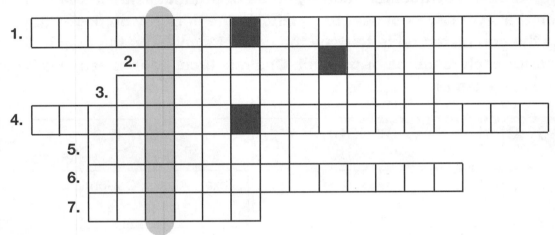

Clues

1 the plant life that grows naturally in an area

2 a group made up of people from the same country, people of the same race, or people with a shared way of life

3 farming

4 industries in which workers are paid to do things for other people

5 the way the people of a region use resources to meet their needs

6 the making of products

7 a usual way of doing things

© Harcourt

Name _____ Date _____

MAP AND GLOBE SKILLS
Use a Land Use and Resource Map

Directions Create a symbol for each resource or product listed in the table below. Then draw your symbol next to its label in the map key on page 23. Finally, use the completed table to draw the correct symbol on the map in the states listed for each resource or product. One resource, natural gas, has been completed as an example.

RESOURCE OR PRODUCT	SYMBOL	STATES
Oil		Texas, Alaska, California
Coal		Wyoming, West Virginia, Kentucky
Natural gas	🔥	Texas, Louisiana, Alaska
Chickens		Georgia, Arkansas, Alabama
Cattle		Texas, Nebraska, Kansas
Fish		Alaska, Louisiana, California
Lumber		Oregon, Washington, California
Cotton		Texas, California, Georgia
Wheat		Kansas, North Dakota, Montana
Corn		Iowa, Illinois, Nebraska
Citrus fruits		Florida, California, Texas

(continued)

Name _____   Date _____

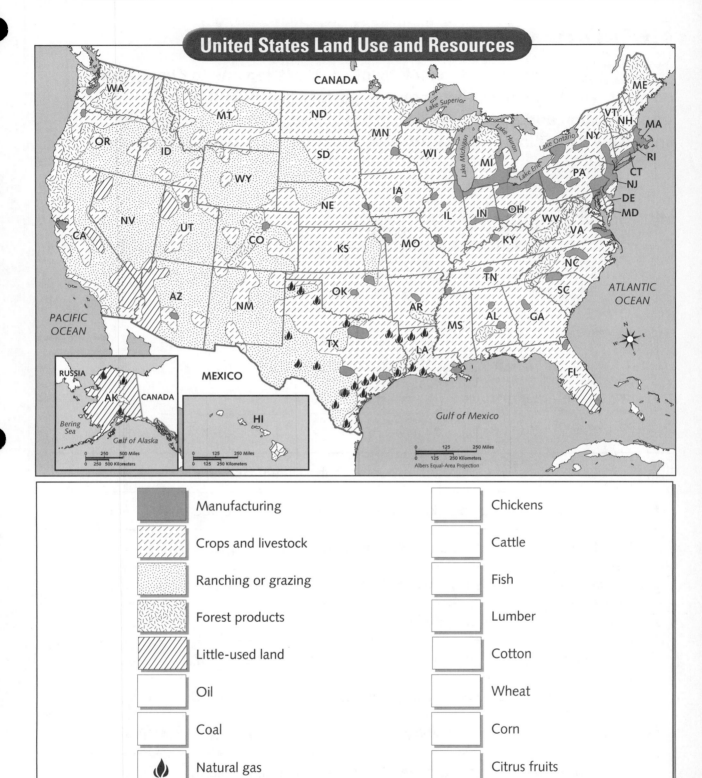

United States Land Use and Resources

Symbol	Resource		Resource
	Manufacturing		Chickens
	Crops and livestock		Cattle
	Ranching or grazing		Fish
	Forest products		Lumber
	Little-used land		Cotton
	Oil		Wheat
	Coal		Corn
	Natural gas		Citrus fruits

Regions Change and Connect

Directions Advances in technology often cause regions to change and connect. The table below lists some important events in the history of transportation and communication in the United States. Complete the time line below by writing the letter of each event from the table at its correct date on the time line.

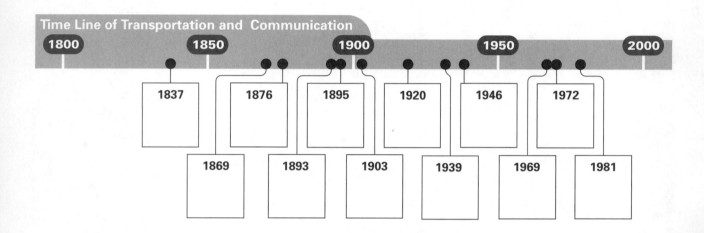

A	In 1939 television broadcasting begins in the United States.
B	The telegraph, which sends messages over wires, is invented in 1837.
C	In 1969 American astronauts become the first people to walk on the moon.
D	Wireless telegraph is invented in 1895.
E	In 1876 the telephone is invented.
F	Electronic mail, or e-mail, is introduced for the Internet in 1972.
G	In 1893 the first gasoline-powered automobile is built in the United States.
H	Coast-to-coast railroad service across the United States begins in 1869.
I	In 1903 Americans conduct the first successful airplane flight.
J	Americans build the first fully electronic digital computer in 1946.
K	Radio broadcasting begins in the United States in 1920.
L	In 1981 the first space shuttle is launched from the United States.

Name _____   Date _____

READING SKILLS

Identify Cause and Effect

Regions of the United States are constantly changing for a variety of reasons. Events and changes that happen in a region sometimes cause other events and changes to take place. Below are some of those events and changes. What caused them? What effects have those causes produced?

Directions Use your textbook's information about different regions in the United States to complete the following cause-and-effect chart.

CAUSE	→	EFFECT

CAUSE		EFFECT
Wind and water wore down the peaks of the Appalachian Mountains over time.	→	_____ _____
_____ _____	→	Silt built up along floodplains and deltas and made the land there very fertile.
People built dams on several rivers in the Phoenix, Arizona, area.	→	_____ _____
_____ _____	→	Tourism became the largest industry in the Orlando, Florida, area.
Cars, trains, airplanes, telephones, computers, and televisions were invented.	→	_____ _____

Use after reading Chapter 2, Skill Lesson, page 78.

Regions Around the World

Directions The facts below describe different kinds of regions around the world. Use pages 79–83 in your textbook to classify the information according to the kind of region that each fact describes. In the blank next to each fact, write *PA* for a physical region of Asia, *CA* for a cultural region of Africa, or *PE* for a political region of Europe.

1 _____ The ten tallest mountains in the world are part of the Himalayas.

2 _____ The Ashanti (uh•SHAN•tee) people of Ghana wear clothes decorated with repeating patterns. The patterns have meanings, which the Ashanti "read" like poems.

3 _____ Vatican City and Monaco are the two smallest countries in the world.

4 _____ During the month-long religious holiday of Ramadan (RAH•muh•dahn), Islamic people fast, or do not eat, during the daytime.

5 _____ The country of Switzerland is divided into 26 regions, called *cantons*, which are similar to our states.

6 _____ So many needleleaf trees cover southern Siberia that people often call the region a "green ocean."

7 _____ The Lingala language of the Congo River area has only one word to mean both "yesterday" and "today." The meaning depends on how people use the word.

8 _____ About four-fifths of the island nation of Indonesia is covered by rain forests.

9 _____ Rome, the capital of Italy, was the first city in the world to have more than 1 million residents.

10 _____ If there were a flight of stairs rising from the bottom of the Dead Sea, you would have to climb about 2,000 steps to reach sea level!

© Harcourt

Looking at Regions

Directions Use this graphic organizer to summarize the main topics of this chapter. For each main topic, write some important details related to the topic. Then write a brief statement to summarize the main idea of the topic.

Looking at Regions

Topic →	Key Facts →	Most Important Information
Place or Event	Who? What? When? Where? Why?	Summary
Kinds of regions		
Regions connect and change		
Regions around the world		

© Harcourt

Name _____ Date _____

2 Test Preparation

Directions Read each question, and choose the best answer. Then fill in the circle for the answer you have chosen. Be sure to fill in the circle completely.

1 Most Americans live in—
- Ⓐ rural regions.
- Ⓑ mountain regions.
- Ⓒ urban regions.
- Ⓓ suburban regions.

2 In what kind of industry do factory workers earn their living?
- Ⓕ manufacturing
- Ⓖ mining
- Ⓗ agriculture
- Ⓙ service

3 Shaking hands when you meet someone is an example of—
- Ⓐ an industry.
- Ⓑ a custom.
- Ⓒ an ethnic group.
- Ⓓ technology.

4 Which of the following is *not* a form of communication?
- Ⓕ telephones
- Ⓖ railroads
- Ⓗ fax machines
- Ⓙ computers

5 What religion do most people in North Africa follow?
- Ⓐ Judaism
- Ⓑ Christianity
- Ⓒ Buddhism
- Ⓓ Islam

© Harcourt

Use after reading Chapter 2, pages 58–83.

New England Through the Years

When the Pilgrims left England, they had planned to settle much farther south along the Atlantic Coast of North America, in what is now Virginia. But the *Mayflower* was blown off course by storms and reached the coast of present-day Massachusetts instead. The Pilgrims decided to make the best of the situation and start their colony there. The first thing they did—even before unloading the ship—was to write and sign the Mayflower Compact to agree on the laws they would all follow.

Directions **Read the contents of the Mayflower Compact below. Then use a dictionary to figure out the meaning of each word in bold print. Match each word to its correct meaning on page 30. Write the word in the blank beside the meaning that fits best. Then answer the questions that follow.**

The Mayflower Compact

In the name of God, Amen. We, whose names are underwritten, the Loyal Subjects of our dread Sovereign Lord, King James, by the Grace of God, of Great Britain, France and Ireland, King, Defender of the Faith, etc.

Having undertaken for the Glory of God, and Advancement of the Christian Faith, and the Honour of our King and Country, a voyage to plant the first colony in the northern Parts of Virginia; do by these Presents, solemnly and **mutually** in the Presence of God and one of another, **covenant** and combine ourselves together into a **civil** Body Politick, for our better Ordering and Preservation, and Furtherance of the Ends aforesaid;

And by Virtue hereof to **enact**, constitute, and frame, such just and equal Laws, **Ordinances**, Acts, **Constitutions** and Offices, from time to time, as shall be thought most meet and convenient for the General Good of the Colony; unto which we promise all due **Submission** and Obedience.

In Witness whereof we have hereunto **subscribed** our names at Cape Cod the eleventh of November, in the Reign of our Sovereign Lord, King James of England, France and Ireland the eighteenth, and of Scotland the fifty-fourth.

Anno Domini, 1620.

© Harcourt

(continued)

1 _____ to make into a law

5 _____ a law or set of laws

2 _____ together, jointly, in common

6 _____ of a community of citizens or their government

3 _____ a plan showing the way in which a government, state, or society is organized

7 _____ the act of giving in to the power of another or others

4 _____ to promise or pledge

8 _____ signed one's name at the end of a document to show consent

9 Where were the Pilgrims when they wrote the Mayflower Compact?

_____

10 On what date did the Pilgrims write that they signed the Mayflower Compact?

_____

11 Who was the king of England and Ireland when the compact was written?

_____

12 In what part of North America did the Pilgrims write that they would "plant the

first colony"? _____

13 What three reasons did the Pilgrims list for voyaging to North America and

starting a colony there? _____

_____

14 What do you think the Pilgrims meant when they said the purpose of the
Mayflower Compact was "for our better Ordering and Preservation" and

"for the General Good of the Colony"? _____

_____

_____

© Harcourt

Use after reading Chapter 3, Lesson 1, pages 100–105.

CHART AND GRAPH SKILLS
Read a Time Line

Many time lines run horizontally from left to right across a page. Other time lines are vertical. A vertical time line lists events in order from top to bottom. The earliest date appears at the top of the time line. The latest date is listed at the bottom of the time line.

Directions Use the time line to answer the following questions.

1 How many years does this time line cover?

_____

2 Into what equal time periods is this time line divided?

_____

3 Which New England state joined the United States first?

_____

4 What was the last New England state to join the United States?

_____

5 In what year did three parts of New England become states?

_____

6 Could you label the founding of Plymouth Colony on this time line? Why or why not?

_____

_____

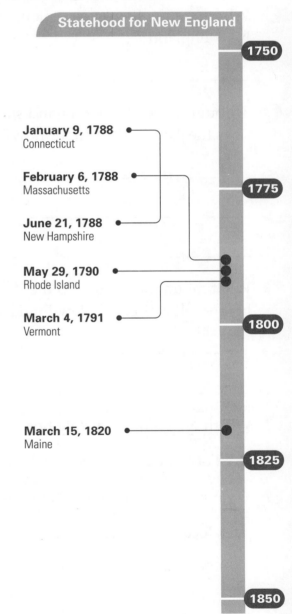

Statehood for New England

1750

January 9, 1788
Connecticut

February 6, 1788
Massachusetts

1775

June 21, 1788
New Hampshire

May 29, 1790
Rhode Island

March 4, 1791
Vermont

1800

March 15, 1820
Maine

1825

1850

© Harcourt

Name _____ Date _____

The New England Countryside

Directions Use the map of New England to answer these questions.

1 What two bodies of water form the southern and eastern boundaries of

New England? _____

_____

2 Where are the lowest elevations in New England?

_____

3 Through which New England states does the Connecticut River flow?

_____

_____

4 What mountains make up the highest elevations in New England?

_____

_____

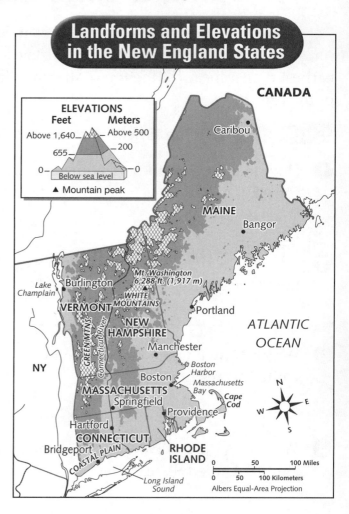

Landforms and Elevations in the New England States

5 Which New England state borders Lake Champlain? What is the elevation of

most of the land around this lake? _____

6 What is the elevation of Mount Washington? In which New England state is this

peak located? _____

Use after reading Chapter 3, Lesson 2, pages 108–111.

© Harcourt

Name _____ Date _____

A New England Town

Directions Complete this table to compare Newfane, Vermont, in the past to Newfane, Vermont, today.

TOPIC	NEWFANE, 1800s	NEWFANE, 2000s
Arrangement of buildings		
Uses of the town common		
The economy		
Transportation and communication		
Local government		

Use after reading Chapter 3, Lesson 3, pages 112–115.

Name _____ Date _____

CITIZENSHIP SKILLS
Solve a Problem

Directions At a recent town meeting, the citizens of Newfane, Vermont, decided how to solve the problem of caring for stray dogs and cats found in their area. Use the graphic organizer below to think of ways to solve the same problem in your community.

IDENTIFY THE PROBLEM.

THINK OF POSSIBLE SOLUTIONS.

COMPARE SOLUTIONS AND SELECT THE BEST ONE.

PLAN HOW TO CARRY OUT THE SOLUTION.

SOLVE THE PROBLEM AND EVALUATE THE SOLUTION.

© Harcourt

Use after reading Chapter 3, Skill Lesson, pages 116–117.

Towns and Villages Around the World

Like many towns in the United States, towns and villages around the world often have town seals that are used on official documents. People in those towns usually design the seals to celebrate the town's history, the people who live there, a special building in town, or an unusual physical feature, industry, or attraction.

Directions Use the lines to the left of each blank circle below to list some features of the town or village that is named. Then use your lists to design town seals for these places in the blank circles.

HAWKSHEAD, ENGLAND

_____

_____

_____

_____

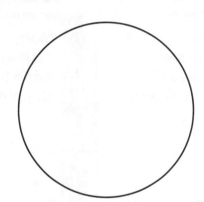

TENTERFIELD, AUSTRALIA

_____

_____

_____

_____

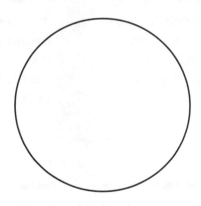

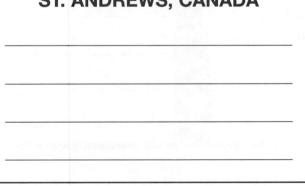

ST. ANDREWS, CANADA

_____

_____

_____

_____

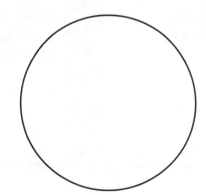

Name _____   Date _____

New England States

Directions Use this graphic organizer to make generalizations about some of the main ideas in the chapter. Read each set of facts about New England. Then make a generalization based on those facts.

New England States

Fact		Fact		Relationship Between Them
FACT 1	**+**	**FACT 2**	**→**	**GENERALIZATION**
New England's first settlements were built on bays along the Atlantic Ocean.	**+**	Many New England settlers made their living in fishing or shipping.	**→**	_____ _____ _____ _____ _____ _____
Much of coastal New England has rocky soil, and it is difficult to grow many crops there.	**+**	Much of the New England countryside has rocky soil, and it is difficult to grow many crops there.	**→**	_____ _____ _____ _____ _____ _____
Many small towns in New England hold town meetings.	**+**	Town meetings allow residents to participate in their local government.	**→**	_____ _____ _____ _____ _____ _____

© Harcourt

Name _____ Date _____

3 Test Preparation

Directions Read each question and choose the best answer. Then fill in the circle for the answer you have chosen. Be sure to fill in the circle completely.

1 The Pilgrims sailed to North America because—
  Ⓐ they were in search of riches.
  Ⓑ they wanted to learn from Native Americans.
  Ⓒ England was too crowded.
  Ⓓ they were not allowed to practice their religion in England.

2 Which of the following is *not* a major crop grown in New England?
  Ⓕ apples
  Ⓖ potatoes
  Ⓗ cotton
  Ⓙ cranberries

3 Stone is mined in a—
  Ⓐ factory.
  Ⓑ quarry.
  Ⓒ glacier.
  Ⓓ common.

4 In what way do people in many New England towns participate in local government?
  Ⓕ by attending town meetings
  Ⓖ by volunteering at fund-raisers
  Ⓗ by working in the tourist industry
  Ⓙ by preserving historical sites

5 Why do people in the United States, Australia, and parts of Canada speak English?
  Ⓐ because each of those places was once a British colony
  Ⓑ because most people in each of those places have English ancestors
  Ⓒ because all of those places border the country of England
  Ⓓ because all of those places are part of the United Kingdom

Use after reading Chapter 3, pages 98–121.

The Middle Atlantic Colonies

By 1775, the year before the American colonists declared their independence from Britain, more than 2 million people lived in the 13 colonies along the Atlantic Coast. Who were the colonists, and where did they come from?

Directions Use the information in the pictograph below to answer the questions that follow.

Ethnic Groups in the 13 Colonies, 1775

ETHNIC GROUP	ESTIMATED POPULATION
English	🧍🧍 🧍🧍🧍🧍🧍🧍🧍🧍🧍🧍🧍🧍🧍🧍🧍🧍🧍🧍🧍🧍🧍🧍🧍
African	🧍
Swedish	🧍🧍
French	🧍🧍🧍🧍
Dutch	🧍🧍🧍🧍🧍🧍🧍
Scottish	🧍🧍🧍🧍🧍🧍🧍🧍🧍🧍🧍🧍🧍🧍🧍🧍
German	🧍🧍🧍🧍🧍🧍🧍🧍🧍🧍🧍🧍🧍🧍🧍🧍
Scotch-Irish	🧍🧍🧍🧍🧍🧍🧍🧍🧍🧍🧍🧍🧍🧍🧍🧍🧍🧍
Other	🧍🧍🧍🧍🧍🧍🧍🧍🧍🧍🧍🧍

🧍 = 500,000 people   🧍 = 10,000 people

1 From what country did almost half of all the colonists come? _____

2 What was the second-largest ethnic group in the colonies in 1775? _____

3 Were there more French colonists or Swedish colonists? _____

4 About how many people from Germany lived in the colonies? _____

_____

5 What does the category "Other" mean in this pictograph?

_____

_____

© Harcourt

READING SKILLS
Identify Fact and Opinion

Directions American colonists made each of the statements below about declaring their independence from Britain. Read each statement, and decide whether it states a fact or an opinion. Write *F* beside a statement of fact, and write *O* beside a statement of opinion.

1 _____ "Yesterday . . . a resolution was passed, without one dissenting colony, that these United Colonies are, and of right ought to be, free and independent States."
—John Adams, Letter to Abigail Adams, Philadelphia, July 3, 1776

2 _____ "These are the times that try men's souls. . . . the harder the conflict, the more glorious the triumph."
—Thomas Paine, *The American Crisis*, December 23, 1776

3 _____ "I know not what course others may take, but as for me, give me liberty or give me death!"
—Patrick Henry, Speech given at the Virginia Convention, March 23, 1775

4 _____ "It has been determined by Congress, that the whole army raised for the defense of the American cause shall be put under my . . . command."
—George Washington, Letter to Martha Washington, Philadelphia, June 18, 1775

5 _____ "We must all hang together, or assuredly we shall all hang separately."
—Benjamin Franklin, Philadelphia, July 4, 1776

6 _____ ". . . whenever any form of government becomes destructive . . . it is the right of the people to alter or to abolish [end] it."
—Thomas Jefferson, *Declaration of Independence*, July 4, 1776

© Harcourt

Name _____ Date _____

Transportation and Growth

Directions Use the map of the Middle Atlantic states to answer these questions.

1. Where is the largest area of manufacturing in the Middle Atlantic region?

_____

_____

2. What fuel resources are found in the Middle Atlantic states?

_____

3. How is most of the land in Delaware used?

_____

4. Where in the Middle Atlantic region are large areas of land used for growing fruits and vegetables?

_____

_____

5. Which Middle Atlantic state has the least forest land?

_____

6. How does this map help explain why a large steel industry developed in western Pennsylvania?

_____

_____

_____

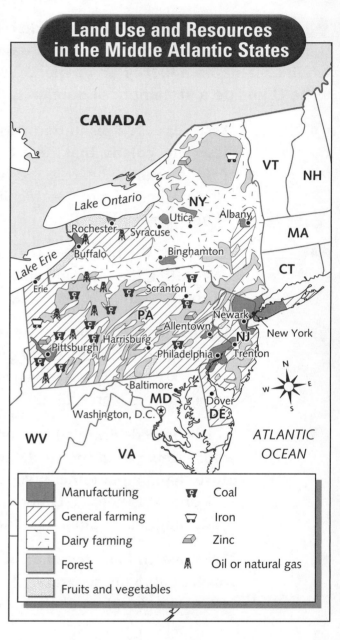

Land Use and Resources in the Middle Atlantic States

CANADA

Lake Ontario

Lake Erie

VT
NH
NY
MA
CT
PA
NJ
MD
DE
WV
VA

Rochester • Syracuse • Utica • Albany
Buffalo • Binghamton
Erie • Scranton
Newark • New York
Allentown
Harrisburg • Trenton
Pittsburgh • Philadelphia
Baltimore
Washington, D.C. • Dover

ATLANTIC OCEAN

Manufacturing		Coal	
General farming		Iron	
Dairy farming		Zinc	
Forest		Oil or natural gas	
Fruits and vegetables			

Use after reading Chapter 4, Lesson 2, pages 134–139.

Name _____ Date _____

MAP AND GLOBE SKILLS
Use a Road Map and Mileage Table

Directions Use the mileage table below and the road map on page 42 to answer these questions.

1. Which interstate highway links Minnesota and Texas? _____

2. Which highway would take you from Los Angeles, California, to Portland, Oregon? What is the mileage between those two places? _____

3. List three cities through which Interstate Highway 80 passes. _____

_____

_____

4. Which east-west interstate highway runs the farthest south? _____

5. If you want to drive from Denver, Colorado, to Kansas City, Missouri, which highway could you take? How many miles would you have to drive?

_____

6. Which highway should you take if you want to start on the Pacific Coast, cross the Rocky Mountains, cross the Mississippi River, travel near the Great Lakes, and end up on the Atlantic Coast? _____

7. What is the mileage between New York City and Miami, Florida? What highway connects those two cities? _____

United States Road Mileage						
	Denver, CO	Kansas City, MO	Los Angeles, CA	Miami, FL	New York City, NY	Portland, OR
Denver, CO		600	1,059	2,066	1,771	1,238
Kansas City, MO	600		1,589	1,464	1,198	1,809
Los Angeles, CA	1,059	1,589		2,735	2,786	959
Miami, FL	2,066	1,464	2,735		1,284	3,260
New York City, NY	1,771	1,198	2,786	1,284		2,855
Portland, OR	1,238	1,809	959	3,260	2,855	

(continued)

© Harcourt

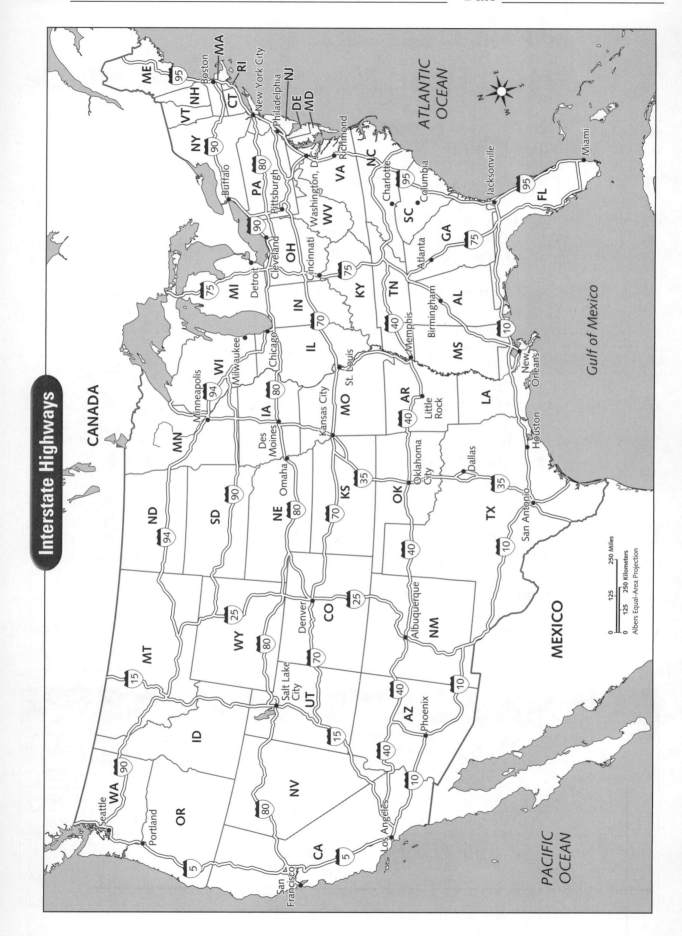

Interstate Highways

Use after reading Chapter 4, Skill Lesson, pages 140–141.

Cities Grow and Change

Directions The following excerpt is from the book *Immigrant Kids* by Russell Freedman. It describes what typical public schools in New York City were like during the early 1900s. Read the excerpt. Then, on the lines below, write a paragraph comparing and contrasting early city schools with your school today.

> Schools had few frills. The school day began with the Pledge of Allegiance. Boys and girls attended separate classes. They came together only in assembly.
>
> Instruction emphasized the three Rs, American history and geography, penmanship, and spelling. Misspelled words were written in a notebook ten times or more. Students memorized long lists of names and dates. They recited to the teacher while standing at attention.

_____

_____

_____

_____

_____

_____

Cities Around the World

Directions Use the maps in your textbook to complete this table. Then use the information in the table to answer the questions that follow.

Largest Urban Areas in the World, 2000			
Urban Area	**Country**	**Continent**	**Population**
Mumbai (Bombay)	India		18,066,000
Buenos Aires	Argentina		12,560,000
Kolkata (Calcutta)	India		12,918,000
Lagos	Nigeria		13,427,000
Los Angeles			13,140,000
Mexico City			18,131,000
New York City			16,640,000
São Paulo	Brazil		17,755,000
Shanghai	China		12,887,000
Tokyo			26,444,000

1 What urban area has the largest population in the world?

_____

2 What are the two largest urban areas in the United States?

_____

3 What is the largest urban area in Africa? How many people live there?

_____

4 How many people live in Mexico City?

_____

5 How many of the ten largest urban areas in the world are located in Asia?

_____

Use after reading Chapter 4, Lesson 4, pages 150–155.

© Harcourt

Middle Atlantic States

Directions Complete this graphic organizer to show that you understand the causes and effects of some of the key events in the history of the Middle Atlantic states.

MIDDLE ATLANTIC STATES

CAUSE	→	EFFECT

Many early settlements in the Middle Atlantic region were built along rivers or near the Atlantic Ocean.

_____
_____
_____
_____

_____
_____
_____
_____

The American colonists became angry about taxation without representation and declared their independence from Britain.

Roads, canals, and railroads were built across the Appalachian Mountains.

_____
_____
_____

_____
_____
_____

Cities in the Middle Atlantic region grew rapidly.

© Harcourt

Name _____ Date _____

Test Preparation

Directions Read each question, and choose the best answer. Then fill in the circle for the answer you have chosen. Be sure to fill in the circle completely.

1 Why did many port cities grow up in the Middle Atlantic region?

 Ⓐ because they were built near the Appalachian Mountains

 Ⓑ because shipbuilding was the largest industry in the region

 Ⓒ because they were built along major rivers near the Atlantic Coast

 Ⓓ because the region was the center for the nation's steel industry

2 Who wrote most of the Declaration of Independence?

 Ⓕ Benjamin Franklin

 Ⓖ Thomas Jefferson

 Ⓗ George Washington

 Ⓙ Thomas Paine

3 People built the Erie Canal to link—

 Ⓐ Lake Erie and the Hudson River.

 Ⓑ Lake Erie and Lake Ontario.

 Ⓒ New York City and Philadelphia.

 Ⓓ the St. Lawrence River and the Atlantic Ocean.

4 Why did many people move to Middle Atlantic cities in the late 1800s and early 1900s?

 Ⓕ to attend colleges and universities

 Ⓖ to buy their own land

 Ⓗ for low-cost housing

 Ⓙ for factory jobs

5 Which of the following is *not* a solution for problems in many urban areas around the world?

 Ⓐ recycling programs

 Ⓑ public transportation

 Ⓒ unemployment

 Ⓓ laws to limit pollution

© Harcourt

Use after reading Chapter 4, pages 124–155.

Settling the Region

Directions Many early settlers along the Fall Line built waterwheels on rivers to run mills that ground wheat into flour. Use this illustration to help you follow the process of using waterpower to produce flour. In each blank, write a number from 1 to 6 to order the steps.

A. _____ The turning of the mill post makes the grinding stone spin.

B. _____ The river water flows over the waterwheel.

C. _____ A stone dam built across the river forces the river water to pour through a small opening.

D. _____ The turning stone grinds the wheat into flour.

E. _____ The force of the rushing river water causes the waterwheel to turn.

F. _____ The turning of the waterwheel causes a post inside the mill to turn.

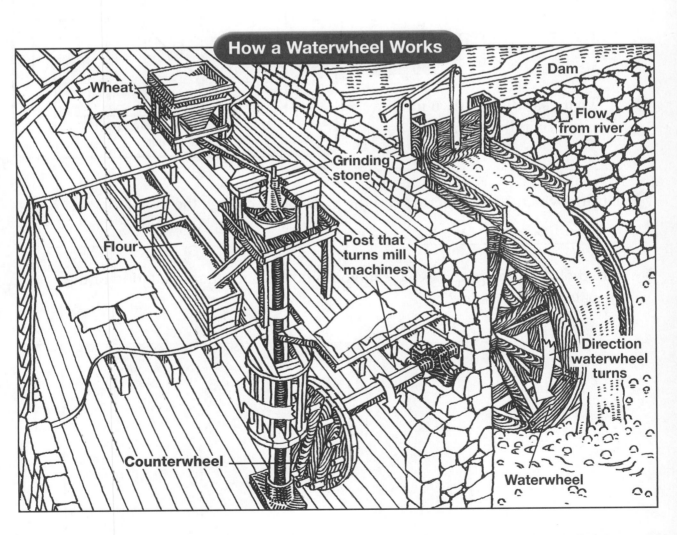

How a Waterwheel Works

CHART AND GRAPH SKILLS
Read a Line Graph

Directions After pioneers cleared the Wilderness Road, thousands of settlers crossed the Appalachian Mountains. As a result, the populations of what are now the Appalachian states of Kentucky, Tennessee, and West Virginia changed rapidly. Use the line graph below to answer the following questions about how the population of those states changed over time.

1 How has the population of the Appalachian states changed in the past 210 years?

_____

2 About how many people lived in the Appalachian states in 1850?

_____

_____

3 In what year did nearly 6 million people live in those states?

_____

_____

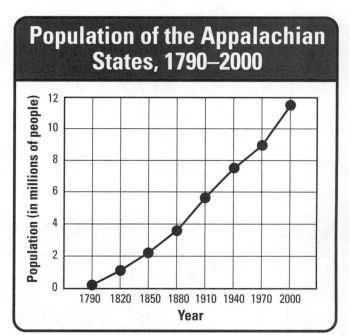

4 During which 30-year period did the population change the most?

_____

5 Based on this line graph, what can you predict about the population of the Appalachian states in 2030?

_____

© Harcourt

Name _____ Date _____

People Use Natural Resources

Directions Complete this graphic organizer to show how natural resources in the Atlantic Coast and Appalachian states are connected to some of the region's industries and products.

NATURAL RESOURCE →	INDUSTRY →	PRODUCT
Fertile soil →	_____ →	Peanuts, soybeans, and cotton
Chesapeake Bay →	Fishing →	_____
_____ →	Manufacturing →	Furniture
Minerals and fuels →	Mining →	_____
_____ →	Agriculture →	Horses
Hydroelectric power →	_____ →	Aluminum
_____ →	Arts and crafts →	Baskets, blankets, pottery, and carvings
Cotton crops →	Manufacturing →	_____

© Harcourt

Cities Grow and Industries Change

Like cities everywhere, cities in the Atlantic Coast and Appalachian region have grown for many different reasons. Some grew because of shipping and trade or new industries. Others grew because they were centers of state and national governments. Still others grew because of the many tourist attractions they offer.

Directions Use pages 186–191 of your textbook to find the names of cities that have grown in the Atlantic Coast and Appalachian region. Then write the names of those cities under the correct headings in the chart below. Some cities may be listed under more than one category.

Atlantic Coast and Appalachian Cities			
CENTERS OF SHIPPING AND TRADE	CENTERS OF NEW INDUSTRIES	CENTERS OF GOVERNMENT	CENTERS OF TOURISM
_____	_____	_____	_____
_____	_____	_____	_____
_____	_____	_____	_____
_____	_____	_____	_____
_____	_____	_____	_____
_____	_____	_____	_____
_____	_____	_____	_____
_____	_____	_____	_____
_____	_____	_____	_____
_____	_____	_____	_____
_____	_____	_____	_____

© Harcourt

Use after reading Chapter 5, Lesson 3, pages 186–191.

National Parks Around the World

Directions Read the descriptions of the national parks below. Then, in the blank next to each park's name, identify what that park preserves or protects. Write *WL* for wildlife, *NR* for natural resources, or *CH* for culture or history.

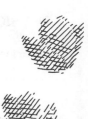

1 _____ **Galápagos National Park, South America** In 1959 Ecuador set aside nearly all of the islands along its Pacific Coast as a national park. Penguins and sea lions live in the park with iguanas and other tropical wildlife. The park's giant tortoises have one of the longest lifespans on Earth—up to 150 years!

2 _____ **Komodo National Park, Asia** The main purpose of this national park in Indonesia is to protect the oldest, largest, and one of the rarest reptiles in the world—the Komodo Dragon. This gigantic reptile lives nowhere else on Earth.

3 _____ **Kakadu National Park, Australia** Scientists in this national park have found evidence of the earliest human settlement in Australia. Some cave paintings there are nearly 20,000 years old! Many sites in the park are of great religious importance to the Aborigines, or the native people of Australia.

4 _____ **Skaftafell National Park, Europe** Founded in 1956, this national park in Iceland preserves an area called the Glacier Country. Visitors to the park can see huge icebergs, ice-blue glacial lakes, shimmering ice tunnels, frozen waterfalls, and miles of thick birch forests.

5 _____ **Garamba National Park, Africa** This park in the Democratic Republic of the Congo protects one of the most endangered animals in the world—the white rhinoceros. Only about 30 of these large animals still survive in the wild. People used to hunt them for their horns, but this is not allowed anymore. In fact, armed guards now protect the white rhinoceroses at the park.

© Harcourt

Atlantic Coast and Appalachian States

Directions Complete this graphic organizer to write facts and opinions about the Atlantic Coast and Appalachian states. For each main topic, write one statement of fact and one statement of opinion.

ATLANTIC COAST AND APPALACHIAN STATES

PHYSICAL FEATURES OF THE ATLANTIC COAST AND APPALACHIAN STATES

FACT: OPINION:

WAYS PEOPLE IN THE ATLANTIC COAST AND APPALACHIAN STATES USE NATURAL RESOURCES TO EARN THEIR LIVING

FACT: OPINION:

REASONS WHY CITIES HAVE GROWN AND OCCUPATIONS HAVE CHANGED IN THE ATLANTIC COAST AND APPALACHIAN STATES

FACT: OPINION:

PURPOSES OF NATIONAL PARKS

FACT: OPINION:

© Harcourt

Name _____   Date _____

5 Test Preparation

Directions Read each question and choose the best answer. Then fill in the circle for the answer you have chosen. Be sure to fill in the circle completely.

1 The first attempt by the English to settle in the Atlantic Coast and Appalachian region took place—
- Ⓐ along the Mississippi River.
- Ⓑ on Roanoke Island.
- Ⓒ on the Cumberland Plateau.
- Ⓓ along the James River.

2 Which of the following is not a mountain range in the Atlantic Coast and Appalachian region?
- Ⓕ Allegheny Mountains
- Ⓖ Blue Ridge Mountains
- Ⓗ Rocky Mountains
- Ⓙ Great Smoky Mountains

3 Why does land often erode after strip mines are used?
- Ⓐ because trees and grasses are removed to mine the coal
- Ⓑ because most of the coal is used to produce electricity
- Ⓒ because deep shafts are dug miles underground
- Ⓓ because large amounts of coal are needed to produce steel

4 Which of these Atlantic Coast and Appalachian cities grew because of state government?
- Ⓕ Memphis, Tennessee
- Ⓖ Louisville, Kentucky
- Ⓗ Chapel Hill, North Carolina
- Ⓙ Richmond, Virginia

5 Which of the following is *not* a purpose of national parks?
- Ⓐ to preserve cultural and historical sites
- Ⓑ to clear more land for farms and industries
- Ⓒ to preserve natural resources
- Ⓓ to protect habitats for special wildlife

Settlement and Early Life

Directions The table below compares the North with the South in 1860. Use the information in the table to answer the questions that follow.

North and South Regions, 1860		
	NORTH	**SOUTH**
Total Population	about 20 million	about 11 million
Enslaved Population	none	about 4 million
Number of Farms of 1,000 Acres or More	about 900	about 4,400
Number of Cities with More Than 10,000 People	77	16
Number of Factories	about 110,000	about 27,000
Number of Factory Workers	about 1,150,000	about 160,000
Annual Value of Factory Products	about $1,660,000,000	about $220,000,000

1 List three details from the table that support the idea that there was more manufacturing in the North than in the South.

_____

_____

_____

2 What information in the table supports the idea that there were more

plantations in the South than in the North? _____

_____

3 Use the facts in the table to make three general statements comparing the population of the North with the population of the South in 1860.

_____

_____

_____

Use after reading Chapter 6, Lesson 1, pages 200–205.

The Southeast and Gulf States Today

Directions Read about how cloth is made from cotton. Then write the numbers from 1 to 8 in the blanks below to put the steps in the correct order.

When cotton is ready to be picked, workers in the fields treat the plants with chemicals to remove the leaves. Then they use farm machines to pick the cotton.

Trucks bring the picked cotton to a processing plant, called a cotton gin. Machines there dry the raw cotton fibers and remove any leaves or other trash. Another machine, called a gin stand, separates the cotton fibers, called lint, from the seeds. Then the lint is cleaned.

A bale press packs the cotton into 500-pound (227-kg) bales, wraps each bale with cloth, and binds it with steel bands. Trucks carry the refrigerator-sized bales to the warehouse. There they are compressed, or squeezed, to about half their size to save space for shipping.

Government inspectors grade samples of the cotton. Growers then sell the graded cotton to brokers, or traders. Brokers, in turn, sell it to cloth manufacturers, who buy large amounts of cotton fiber for their textile factories.

When the cotton arrives at the textile factory, the bales are broken open, and machines clean the lint again and roll it into a long sheet. Then spinning machines separate and straighten the cotton fibers. Other machines twist the fibers into fine, strong thread.

Mechanical looms weave the thread into cloth. Often the cloth is dyed, or colored. Sometimes it is printed, or stamped with a pattern. The cloth manufacturer then sells the finished cotton cloth to clothing manufacturers, who cut and sew the cloth to make items of clothing.

A. _____ The cloth is dyed and printed.

B. _____ Mechanical looms weave the cotton thread into cloth.

C. _____ Chemicals remove the leaves from the plants, and the cotton is picked.

D. _____ The cotton is packed into 500-pound (227-kg) bales.

E. _____ Cloth manufacturers buy the cotton from brokers.

F. _____ Spinning machines separate and straighten the cotton fibers.

G. _____ At the cotton gin, the cotton lint is separated from the seeds.

H. _____ The cotton fibers are twisted into fine, strong thread.

Name _____   Date _____

MAP AND GLOBE SKILLS

Compare Maps with Different Scales

Many of the Civil War's major battles were fought in the Southeast and Gulf states. Early in the war, the Confederates won several important victories. By 1863, however, the Union was winning more battles. One of the Union's most important victories came at Vicksburg, Mississippi. Union guns pounded the city for weeks before the Confederate army surrendered. With this victory, the Union gained control of the Mississippi River. The next year, the Union army marched south from Tennessee into Georgia. After capturing and burning Atlanta, Georgia, the army continued toward Savannah, destroying nearly everything in its path. This march became known as the March to the Sea.

Directions **Use the maps on page 57 to answer the following questions.**

1 About how many miles was the Union army's March to the Sea? About how

many kilometers? _____

2 Which map would you use to find the distance between Vicksburg, Mississippi,

and Atlanta, Georgia? _____

3 About how many miles separate Vicksburg and Jackson, Mississippi? Which

map did you use to answer this question? _____

4 Was the Battle of Vicksburg fought in Union or Confederate territory? Which

map did you use to answer this question? _____

5 How do you think the uses of Map A compare to the uses of Map B?

_____

_____

_____

_____

(continued)

© Harcourt

Name _____ Date _____

Map A: Battle of Vicksburg, 1863

Haynes' Bluff
Snyder's Bluff

MISSISSIPPI

Vanguard Leaves
Milliken's Bend
March 31

Vicksburg, Shreveport & Texas R.R.

New Orleans, Jackson & Great Northern R.R.

Battle of the
Big Black River Bridge
May 17

Richmond   Duckport

VICKSBURG

Southern R.R. of Mississippi   Clinton   Jackson

Edwards
Station

Siege of
Vicksburg
May 18–July 4

Battle of
Champion Hill
May 16   Raymond

Battle of
Jackson
May 14

Mississippi River

Bayou Macon

LOUISIANA

Brierfield

Big Black River

Battle of
Raymond
May 12

Tensas River

Arrives at Hard Times
April 28

Hard
Times

Union Fleet
Bombards
Grand Gulf
April 29

Big Bayou Pierre

Pearl River

Crosses Mississippi River
at Bruinsburg
April 30

Grand
Gulf

Bruinsburg   Port Gibson

Battle of
Port Gibson
May 1

Little Bayou Pierre

→ Grant's march
ⅢⅢⅢⅢ Confederate defenses

0   10   20 Miles
0   10   20 Kilometers

Map B: Major Battles of the Civil War

IOWA

PENNSYLVANIA

Antietam
(Sharpsburg)
1862

Gettysburg
1863

NEW JERSEY

OHIO

ILLINOIS   INDIANA

DELAWARE

Bull Run (Manassas)
1861, 1862

Washington, D.C.

MARYLAND

Ohio River

WEST
VIRGINIA
(1863)

VIRGINIA

Richmond

Chancellorsville 1863

Fredericksburg 1862
Cold Harbor 1864
Seven Days 1862

MISSOURI

Perryville
1862

KENTUCKY

Appomattox
Court House

Petersburg
1864–1865

ATLANTIC
OCEAN

Fort Donelson
1862

Nashville
1864

TENNESSEE

Chattanooga
1863

NORTH
CAROLINA

Wilmington

Franklin
1864

Chickamauga
1863

ARKANSAS

Shiloh
(Pittsburg
Landing)
1862

Mississippi River

Kennesaw
Mountain
1864

SOUTH
CAROLINA

Fort Sumter 1861

Atlanta 1864

Charleston

MISSISSIPPI   ALABAMA

Montgomery

GEORGIA

Fort Wagner 1863

Savannah

0   50   100 Miles
0   50   100 Kilometers
Albers Equal-Area Projection

LOUISIANA

Vicksburg
1863

New Orleans

Mobile

Mobile Bay
1864

New Orleans 1862   Gulf of Mexico

FLORIDA

Union state
Confederate state
Border state
Union blockade
Union victory
Confederate victory
Sherman's March to
the Sea
Capital city

Islands and People

Directions Read the islanders' descriptions of their homes. Then write the letter of the correct island or islands in the blank next to each description. Some letters may be used more than once.

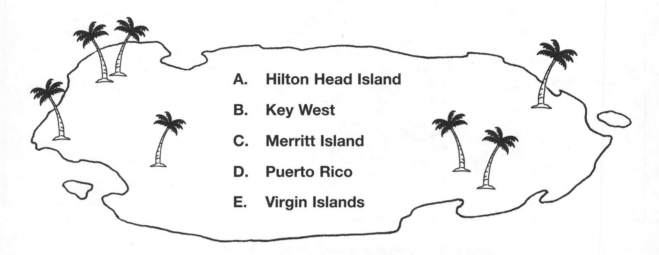

A. **Hilton Head Island**

B. **Key West**

C. **Merritt Island**

D. **Puerto Rico**

E. **Virgin Islands**

1 _____ "The language of my home island is Spanish, but I am an American citizen. My island's name means 'Rich Port' in Spanish."

2 _____ "I work in a hotel on this barrier island off the coast of South Carolina. It is a popular vacation resort, especially for golfers."

3 _____ "My home is one of the coral islands that lie off the coast of Florida. I work as a diver searching for shipwrecks along the reefs surrounding the island."

4 _____ "My family has lived on these islands for many years. I live on St. Croix, my parents live on St. Thomas, and my brother lives on St. John."

5 _____ "I work at the John F. Kennedy Space Center on this barrier island off the east coast of Florida."

6 _____ "My island was linked to the mainland by a railroad, but a hurricane destroyed the tracks in 1935. Today more than 100 miles (160 km) of overseas highway connects my home and the mainland."

7 _____ "Mountains, valleys, beaches, swamps, and rain forests are all within a day's car ride from my house on this island."

8 _____ "The United States purchased my islands from Denmark in 1917, and we have been a United States territory ever since."

© Harcourt

Use after reading Chapter 6, Lesson 3, pages 214–219.

Coastal Regions Around the World

Directions Number the countries in this table from 1 through 10 to put their coastlines in order from longest (1) to shortest (10). Locate each country on the world map on page 60. Then complete the activities at the bottom of this page.

World's Longest Coastlines		
RANK	**COUNTRY**	**LENGTH (in miles)**
	Australia	16,007
	Canada	151,485
	China	9,010
	Indonesia	33,999
	Japan	18,486
	New Zealand	9,404
	Norway	13,624
	Philippines	22,559
	Russia	23,396
	United States	12,380

1 Write each country's coastline rank number at its location on the map.

2 Use the map to find which countries listed in the table border the Atlantic Ocean. Shade those countries blue.

3 Use a different color to shade those countries that are an island or that are made up entirely of several islands.

4 Write **X** on the countries that are located in North America.

5 Write **Y** on the countries that border both the Indian Ocean and the Pacific Ocean.

(continued)

Major Coastal Countries of the World

PACIFIC OCEAN

JAPAN

PHILIPPINES

NEW ZEALAND

AUSTRALIA

INDONESIA

CHINA

RUSSIA

INDIAN OCEAN

NORWAY

ARCTIC OCEAN

ATLANTIC OCEAN

CANADA

UNITED STATES

PACIFIC OCEAN

40°N
80°N
180°
140°E
100°E
60°E
20°E
20°W
60°W
100°W
140°W
180°
80°N
40°N

0°
40°S
180°
140°E
100°E
60°E
20°E
20°W
60°W
100°W
140°W
80°S

Arctic Circle
Tropic of Cancer
Equator
Tropic of Capricorn
40°S
Antarctic Circle

0   1000   2000 Miles
0   1000   2000 Kilometers
Robinson Projection
Scale accurate at equator

Use after reading Chapter 6, Lesson 4, pages 220–225.

Southeast and Gulf States

Directions Complete this graphic organizer to compare and contrast the Southeast and Gulf states.

THE SOUTHEAST AND GULF STATES

Southeast States   **Gulf States**

DIFFERENCES

1. _____

_____

2. _____

_____

3. _____

_____

4. _____

_____

SIMILARITIES

1. _____

_____

2. _____

_____

3. _____

_____

4. _____

_____

DIFFERENCES

1. _____

_____

2. _____

_____

3. _____

_____

4. _____

_____

Name _____ Date _____

6 Test Preparation

Directions Read each question and choose the best answer. Then fill in the circle for the answer you have chosen. Be sure to fill in the circle completely.

1. Which European country was the first to claim land in the Southeast and Gulf region?
   - (A) England
   - (B) France
   - (C) Spain
   - (D) Holland

2. Why is cotton a major crop in the Southeast and Gulf region?
   - (F) because the region has a long growing season and plentiful rainfall
   - (G) because the region borders the Atlantic Ocean
   - (H) because the Mississippi River forms the region's western boundary
   - (J) because farming is the largest industry in the region

3. The Florida Keys are made up of—
   - (A) the peaks of mountain ranges.
   - (B) layers of coral and limestone.
   - (C) sand, shells, and soil.
   - (D) rain forests and swamps.

4. Which of the following is a major port city along the Gulf of Mexico?
   - (F) Miami, Florida
   - (G) Charleston, South Carolina
   - (H) Mobile, Alabama
   - (J) Savannah, Georgia

5. Which of the following countries around the world does not have coastal regions?
   - (A) Greece
   - (B) Brazil
   - (C) Switzerland
   - (D) India

© Harcourt

Use after reading Chapter 6, pages 198–225.

Settling the South Central Region

In 1830 the United States government passed the Indian Removal Act. This act said that all Native Americans living east of the Mississippi River must leave their lands and move west to the Indian Territory, in what is today Oklahoma. Many tribes fought against the removal, but by 1838, soldiers had forced nearly all of the Indians off their lands. More than 4,000 Cherokees died of cold, disease, and lack of food during their 116-day march to the Indian Territory. The Cherokees called their long, painful journey the "Trail Where They Cried." It later became known as the Trail of Tears.

Directions **Use the map to answer the following questions.**

1 In which present-day state did the Trail of Tears end?

_____

2 Through which present-day states were the Cherokees forced to march?

_____

_____

3 What rivers did they have to cross during the journey?

_____

4 Why do you think this event in American history is known as the Trail of Tears?

_____

_____

_____

_____

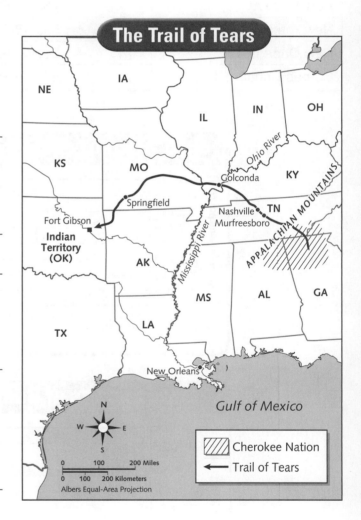

The Trail of Tears

© Harcourt

Name _____ Date _____

A Diverse Economy

Directions The table below shows the amount of exports and imports that each of the nation's five busiest ports handles each year. Use the information in the table to complete the two bar graphs that follow.

Busiest Ports in the United States		
PORT	IMPORTS (in tons per year)	EXPORTS (in tons per year)
Port of South Louisiana, LA	30,602,117	57,419,203
Houston, TX	75,118,513	33,431,259
New York, NY and NJ	53,518,545	8,028,061
New Orleans, LA	26,383,831	21,731,316
Corpus Christi, TX	52,595,352	7,635,218

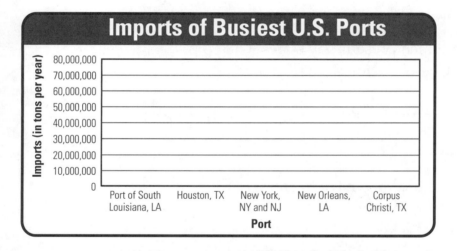

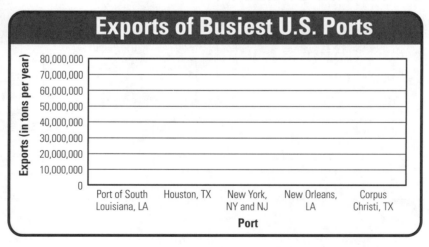

Use after reading Chapter 7, Lesson 2, pages 236–241.

© Harcourt

Sharing a River

Directions The United States–Mexico border extends about 2,067 miles (3,326 km) across North America. As a result, the two countries share many physical features. Use the map below to answer the questions that follow.

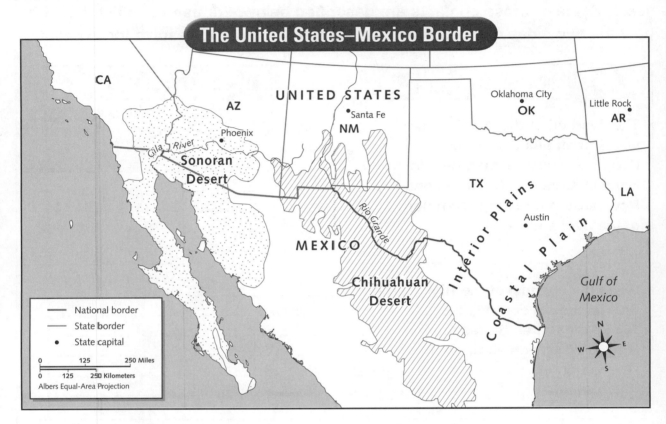

The United States–Mexico Border

1️⃣ What two major rivers do the United States and Mexico share?

_____

2️⃣ What two large desert regions cover parts of both Mexico and the United States? Which of those deserts covers part of the South Central region?

_____

3️⃣ What two plains regions extend from the South Central states into Mexico?

_____

4️⃣ What major body of water forms the eastern boundary of Mexico and the southeastern boundary of the South Central region of the United States?

_____

Name _____ Date _____

CITIZENSHIP SKILLS
Resolve Conflicts

Directions Sharing the Rio Grande has caused several conflicts over the years. Some of those conflicts are described below. For each conflict, describe how the two sides compromised and worked together to resolve the conflict.

CONFLICT	RESOLUTION
The riverbed of the Rio Grande was sometimes dry in Texas. People in Texas blamed people living upstream in Colorado and New Mexico for using too much of the river's water.	
When the channel of the Rio Grande moved south in the 1860s, the United States and Mexico disagreed about their shared border.	
Millions of people in Mexico depend on the Rio Grande for water. The way the river is used upstream in the United States affects Mexico's use of the river.	
Economic development and population growth along the Rio Grande in both Mexico and the United States increased pollution in the river.	

© Harcourt

Oil Resources Around the World

Millions of years ago, oceans covered even more of Earth's surface than they do today. As tiny sea creatures died, their remains sank to the bottoms of the oceans. Over time, the mud and sand that covered the creatures hardened into rock. These layers of rock pressed down on the sea creatures' remains, turning them into oil. In fact, much of the world's oil lies buried hundreds of feet below the surface of the ocean. To reach and remove this oil, people build offshore oil rigs.

Directions The drawing on page 68 is a cross-section diagram of an offshore oil rig. It shows what you would see if you could slice through the ocean and then look at the cut surface. Use the diagram to answer the following questions about how an offshore oil rig works.

1 What parts of an offshore oil rig hold the derrick and other equipment above the ocean water?

_____

2 What materials make up the layers separating the ocean waters from the oil deposits? Which of those materials is a fuel resource?

_____

3 What equipment digs a hole through those layers to reach the oil?

_____

4 Where on the offshore rig does the oil go after it is brought up through pipes from the ocean floor?

_____

5 How does the oil get from the offshore oil rig to refineries on the mainland?

_____

6 How do you think workers get to their jobs on offshore oil rigs?

_____

_____

(continued)

An Offshore Oil Rig

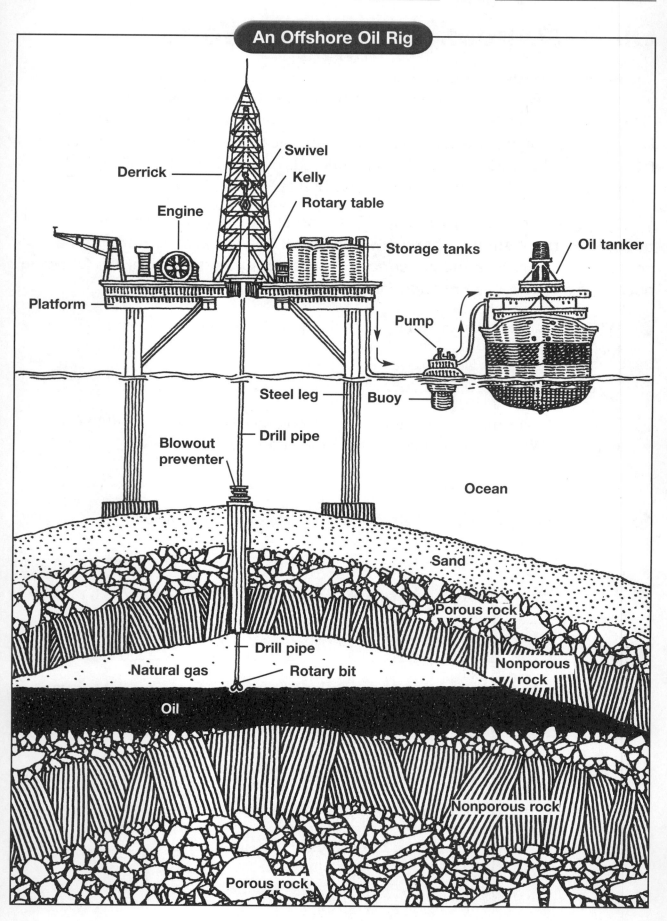

Derrick

Swivel

Kelly

Engine

Rotary table

Storage tanks

Oil tanker

Platform

Pump

Steel leg

Buoy

Drill pipe

Blowout preventer

Ocean

Sand

Porous rock

Nonporous rock

Drill pipe

Natural gas

Rotary bit

Oil

Nonporous rock

Porous rock

© Harcourt

Use after reading Chapter 7, Lesson 4, pages 248–251.

South Central States

Directions Use this graphic organizer to categorize information about the South Central states. Complete it by listing two facts for each subject category.

GEOGRAPHY

1. _____

_____

_____

_____

2. _____

_____

_____

_____

HISTORY

1. _____

_____

_____

_____

2. _____

_____

_____

_____

SOUTH CENTRAL STATES

ECONOMY

1. _____

_____

_____

_____

2. _____

_____

_____

_____

CULTURE

1. _____

_____

_____

_____

2. _____

_____

_____

_____

Use after reading Chapter 7, pages 228–251.

Name _____ Date _____

7 Test Preparation

Directions Read each question and choose the best answer. Then fill in the circle for the answer you have chosen. Be sure to fill in the circle completely.

1. Near what present-day city did Spanish colonists from Mexico build their first settlement in the South Central region?
   - Ⓐ New Orleans, Louisiana
   - Ⓑ Houston, Texas
   - Ⓒ El Paso, Texas
   - Ⓓ Tulsa, Oklahoma

2. Many bayous are located in the—
   - Ⓕ Ozark Plateau.
   - Ⓖ Chihuahuan Desert.
   - Ⓗ Great Plains.
   - Ⓙ Mississippi Delta.

3. Why did early Texas ranchers drive their cattle north to towns in Missouri, Kansas, and Nebraska?
   - Ⓐ to reach better grazing land
   - Ⓑ to ship the cattle to markets on railroads
   - Ⓒ to trade for horses at larger ranches
   - Ⓓ to reach rivers so their cattle would have drinking water

4. Which of the following industries is *not* a major part of the South Central region's diverse economy?
   - Ⓕ mining silver and gold
   - Ⓖ shipping and trading goods
   - Ⓗ drilling and refining oil
   - Ⓙ growing cotton and rice

5. The world's leading producer of oil is—
   - Ⓐ Nigeria.
   - Ⓑ Russia.
   - Ⓒ Saudi Arabia.
   - Ⓓ the United States.

Use after reading Chapter 7, pages 228–251.

Name _____ Date _____

The Old Northwest

Directions The following excerpt is from *Abraham Lincoln: A First Book* by Larry Metzger. It describes what life was like for settlers moving to the Northwest Territory. Read the excerpt. Then answer the questions that follow.

Moving on the frontier was a difficult business. The Lincolns walked the entire way, because they carried things like pots, pans, and a spinning wheel on their horses and in their wagon. They traveled over 100 miles (160 km) on foot, crossing the mighty Ohio River and cutting their way through the heavy forest on the other side....

Winter was a bad time to be settling into a new home in the wilderness.... The Lincolns had to build some kind of shelter quickly.... Thomas [Lincoln's father] was a skilled carpenter who had built several cabins before, and Abraham was able to help by clearing brush and by trimming branches from the logs that were used to make the cabin walls.... The Lincolns heated their home by burning wood in a stone fireplace, and they filled the spaces between the logs with mud and grass in order to keep out the wind....

When spring came that year, it was time for the family to clear the trees and brush so they could start a farm. This was hard work, because the land was heavily wooded and they had only axes to do the job. Even though Abraham was only eight years old, he helped his father chop down trees and split logs for firewood and fence rails.

After they cleared the land, Abraham and his father plowed the soil and planted corn. When the corn ripened, Abraham helped harvest it and carry it to the mill, where it was ground into flour.

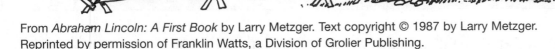

From *Abraham Lincoln: A First Book* by Larry Metzger. Text copyright © 1987 by Larry Metzger. Reprinted by permission of Franklin Watts, a Division of Grolier Publishing.

1 How did the Lincolns reach their new home in the Northwest Territory?

_____

_____

2 What natural resources did the Lincolns use for their new home? _____

_____

3 What kind of work did Abraham do to help his family survive on the frontier?

_____

_____

Name _____ Date _____

MAP AND GLOBE SKILLS
Compare Historical Maps

Directions The French and Indian War began in 1754 and ended in 1763. The two historical maps below show the different countries that claimed land in North America before and after the war. Use the maps to answer the questions.

1. Which country claimed more land in North America in 1763, the British or the French? _____

2. How did Spanish claims to land in North America change after the French and Indian War? _____

_____

3. How did the French and Indian War affect control of the Great Lakes region?

_____

_____

Use after reading Chapter 8, Skill Lesson, pages 274–275.

Life in the Great Lakes Region

Directions Use the information in this table about the Great Lakes to answer the questions that follow.

Facts about the Great Lakes					
LAKE	**Erie**	**Huron**	**Michigan**	**Ontario**	**Superior**
ORIGIN OF NAME	Iroquois Indian for "cat"	Huron Indians	Ojibwa Indian for "great lake"	Iroquois for "beautiful lake"	French for "greatest"
AREA in square miles (sq km)	9,910 (25,667)	23,000 (59,570)	22,400 (58,016)	7,600 (19,684)	31,800 (82,362)
BORDERS	Michigan, New York, Ohio, Pennsylvania, Canada	Michigan, Canada	Illinois, Indiana, Michigan, Wisconsin	New York, Canada	Michigan, Minnesota, Wisconsin, Canada
MAJOR U.S. PORTS	Buffalo, Cleveland, Erie, Toledo	Bay City, Port Huron	Chicago, Gary, Milwaukee	Oswego, Rochester	Duluth, Superior

1 Which Great Lakes names originate from Native American languages?

_____

2 What is the largest Great Lake? the smallest?

_____

3 What is the only Great Lake that does *not* border any of the Great Lakes states?

_____

4 What are some major port cities along Lake Michigan?

_____

Use after reading Chapter 8, Lesson 2, pages 276–280.

Name _____ Date _____

River Transportation

Directions This map shows some of the towns and cities that grew up along rivers in the Middle West region of the United States. Study the map. Then answer the questions that follow.

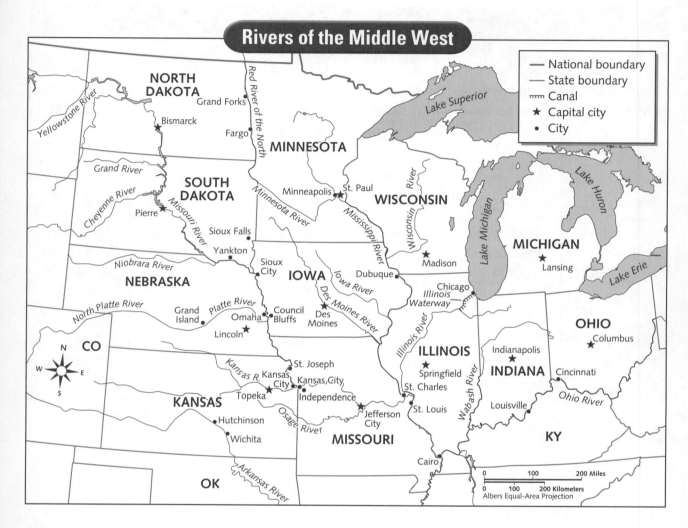

Rivers of the Middle West

1. Which capital cities in the Middle West region are located along rivers?

   _____

2. Which river forms part of the border between Illinois and Indiana?

   _____

3. Into what large river does the Platte River flow? _____

(continued)

Use after reading Chapter 8, Lesson 3, pages 281–285.

© Harcourt

4 Imagine that you are traveling by river in the Middle West region. According to the map, which river or rivers could you use if you were going from

    a. Cincinnati, Ohio, to St. Louis, Missouri?

    _____

    b. St. Joseph, Missouri, to Sioux City, Iowa?

    _____

    c. Chicago, Illinois, to Cairo, Illinois?

    _____

    d. Minneapolis, Minnesota, to Des Moines, Iowa?

    _____

5 What are two tributaries of the Missouri River that flow through South Dakota?

_____

6 Which rivers in the Middle West region share their names with Middle West

states? _____

_____

7 Which two Middle West states have cities named Kansas City? What two rivers

meet near those two cities? _____

_____

8 How are boats from Lake Michigan able to reach rivers in the Middle West

region? _____

_____

Name _____ Date _____

Rivers Around the World

Directions Read the sentences below about rivers around the world. Then select the words from the boats to correctly complete each sentence.

1 The _____ is the most important source of fresh water in Egypt.

2 A tropical location and high precipitation levels have produced the world's

largest _____ along the _____.

3 For Hindus, the _____ is a holy river.

4 Farmers in China grow tons of rice in _____ stretching from the

banks of the _____.

5 The _____ stops the Nile River from flooding and supplies fresh
water and electricity for people and industries.

6 From its _____ in the mountains of Peru, the Amazon River flows
east across Brazil to the Atlantic Ocean.

7 Industries in many European countries use the _____ to transport

raw materials and finished products to the ocean port of _____.

Use after reading Chapter 8, Lesson 4, pages 286–290.

Name _____ Date _____

 CITIZENSHIP SKILLS
Make a Thoughtful Decision

Directions Think about a decision you made recently in school. Then use the graphic organizer below to record and analyze your decision-making process. Fill in as many possible actions and consequences as you can.

GOAL

_____
_____
_____
_____

POSSIBLE ACTIONS	POSSIBLE CONSEQUENCES
1 _____	1 _____
2 _____	2 _____
3 _____	3 _____
4 _____	4 _____

YOUR CHOICE	REASONS FOR YOUR CHOICE
_____	_____
_____	_____
_____	_____

THE RESULT OF YOUR CHOICE

_____
_____
_____

© Harcourt

Great Lakes States

Directions Use this graphic organizer to sequence events that have occurred in the Great Lakes states. Complete it by writing the event in the appropriate date's box.

GREAT LAKES STATES

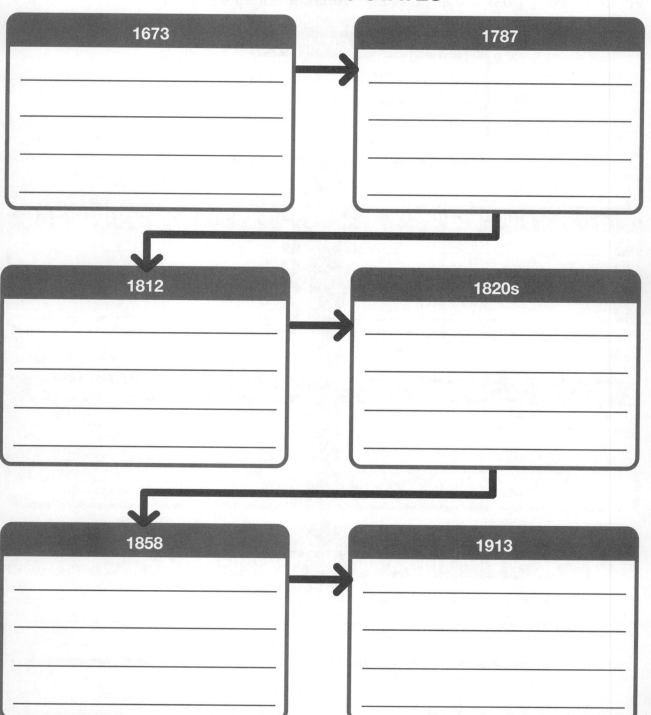

Use after reading Chapter 8, pages 266–291.

Name _____ Date _____

8 Test Preparation

Directions Read each question and choose the best answer. Then fill in the circle for the answer you have chosen. Be sure to fill in the circle completely.

1 After which war did the United States gain control of most of the Great Lakes region?
- Ⓐ the American Revolution
- Ⓑ the Civil War
- Ⓒ the French and Indian War
- Ⓓ the War of 1812

2 The Northwest Territory was divided into squares called—
- Ⓕ ordinances.
- Ⓖ townships.
- Ⓗ territories.
- Ⓙ frontiers.

3 Which of the following is *not* a major reason why the automobile industry grew in the Great Lakes region?
- Ⓐ The region has many navigable waterways to ship goods.
- Ⓑ Factory owners in the region used mass production to produce cars.
- Ⓒ The region's steel industry provided materials needed to manufacture cars.
- Ⓓ People buy more cars in this region than anywhere else in the country.

4 On what kind of boats are most goods shipped on the Mississippi River today?
- Ⓕ barges
- Ⓖ steamboats
- Ⓗ flatboats
- Ⓙ keelboats

5 Along which river would you see miles and miles of rice paddies?
- Ⓐ the Ganges River
- Ⓑ the Chang Jiang
- Ⓒ the Amazon River
- Ⓓ the Nile River

© Harcourt

Early Days on the Interior Plains

Directions The following excerpt is from *Frontier Living* by Edwin Tunis. Read the excerpt. Then complete the activities that follow.

A family couldn't live forever in its wagon, and the Homestead Act required a house; but there wasn't enough wood for a house. The Mandan and the Pawnee Indians solved the problem with earth lodges and the white men did the same; they cut the sod into blocks and laid up walls with it as bricks are laid. . . . If they could find a bank [slope or hill], they dug the back of the house into it, building only the front and part of the side walls of sod [to make a dugout]. Poles for roof rafters came from a river bank and on them the builders spread brush, grass, and more sod. The floor was dirt. Canvas or leather made a door, and anything but glass covered a window. . . . The roofs . . . leaked so badly that people customarily hung small tents over their beds. Even in dry weather, dirt from the roof got over and into everything. . . . there were also bugs and mice and sometimes a cow wandered onto a dugout roof and suddenly joined the family below [when the roof collapsed].

From *Frontier Living* by Edwin Tunis. Text copyright © 1961 by Edwin Tunis. Published by HarperCollins Publishers. Reprinted by permission of Curtis Brown, Ltd.

1 Why did pioneers on the Great Plains build sod houses? _____

_____

2 List the steps a pioneer family followed to build a sod house. _____

_____

_____

3 On a separate sheet of paper, describe how you would feel if you lived in a sod house. How would living in such a house be different from where you live today? What are some items in your home that you would find it difficult to live without in a sod house? _____

_____

© Harcourt

Use after reading Chapter 9, Lesson 1, pages 296–301.

Name _____ Date _____

MAP AND GLOBE SKILLS
Use a Cultural Map

Directions Use the map on page 82 to answer the questions below.

1 What Native American groups labeled on the map were part of the Plains culture?

_____

2 What tribes labeled on the map lived along the shores of the Great Lakes?

_____

_____

3 How do you think life for Caribbean Native American groups differed from life for Arctic Native American groups? _____

_____

4 In what cultural region did the Aztec Indians live? _____

5 Which Native American group or groups lived where your state is today?

_____

6 What connection do you see between the names of the Native American cultural groups on the map and the names of places in the United States today?

_____

_____

(continued)

Name _____ Date _____

Early Cultures of North America

ASIA

ARCTIC OCEAN

INUPIAT
YUP'IK
ALEUT
ATHABASKAN
HAN
INUIT
INUIT
INUIT
INUIT
INUIT
KASKA
TLINGIT
HAIDA
CHIPEWYAN
Hudson Bay
NASKAPI
BEOTHUK
BELLA COOLA
CREE
CREE
CREE
MICMAC
NOOTKA
KOOTENAI
BLACKFOOT
CREE
PENOBSCOT
MAKAH
CHINOOK
ASSINIBOINE
OJIBWA
OJIBWA
ALGONKIN
PACIFIC OCEAN
YAKIMA
NEZ PERCE
CROW
MANDAN
CHIPPEWA
OTTAWA
HURON
MASSACHUSET
ERIE IROQUOIS
IROQUOIS LEAGUE
CAYUGA
MOHAWK
ONEIDA
ONONDAGA
SENECA
POMO
PAIUTE
SHOSHONE
KAW
CHEYENNE
SIOUX
SIOUX
SAUK FOX
DELAWARE
SHOSHONE
UTE
PAWNEE
IOWA
MIAMI
POWHATAN
YOKUTS
PAIUTE
ARAPAHO
MISSOURI
ILLINOIS
SHAWNEE
CHUMASH
APACHE
OSAGE
TUSCARORA
ATLANTIC OCEAN
HOPI
NAVAJO
PUEBLO
ACOMA
ZUNI
KIOWA
QUAPAW
YUCHI
CHICKASAW
CHEROKEE
TOHO NO-O-OTAM
APACHE
COMANCHE
CADDO
CHOCTAW
NATCHEZ
YAQUI
TIMUCUA
CALUSA
COAHUILTEC
Gulf of Mexico
CIBONEY
TAINO
ARAWAK
HUICHOL
CIBONEY
TOLTEC
AZTEC
MAYA
Carribbean Sea
MIXTEC
ZAPOTEC
MOSQUITO
SOUTH AMERICA

0   300   600 Miles
0   300   600 Kilometers
Azimuthal Equal-Area Projection

Legend:
- Arctic
- Subarctic
- Northwest Coast
- Plateau
- California
- Great Basin
- Southwest
- Plains
- Eastern Woodlands
- Middle America
- Caribbean
- Present-day border

© Harcourt

Farming and Ranching on the Plains

Directions Read the information at the bottom of this page and on page 84 about some famous entrepreneurs in American history. Then fill in the missing information in the chart below. Use your textbook to find the information for Joseph McCoy.

Entrepreneur	Company and Product or Service It Supplied	Demand the Business Met
Joyce C. Hall		
John Harvey Kellogg		
Joseph McCoy		
Richard W. Sears		
Levi Strauss		
Sarah Walker		

Joyce C. Hall grew up in Nebraska in the late 1800s. He used money he had earned during high school to start a greeting card business in Kansas City, Missouri, in 1910. Hall helped create the modern greeting-card industry by being one of the first people to sell inexpensive cards with matching envelopes instead of the postcards and elaborate valentines common at the time. Today, Hallmark Cards, Inc., is the largest greeting-card manufacturer in the world.

(continued)

© Harcourt

John Harvey Kellogg was an American doctor and health-food pioneer during the late 1800s. Kellogg was once sued by a woman who broke her false teeth on the hard bread that he had recommended she should eat each morning. Because of this incident, Kellogg decided to produce a softer, healthful, ready-to-eat breakfast food. The result was the world's first dry cereal, which today is known as Kellogg's Corn Flakes.

Richard W. Sears began working as a station agent for the Minneapolis and St. Louis Railway in the 1880s. While working, he saw a great demand for manufactured products in the rural Middle West, where there were few stores. So Sears started a mail-order business with his partner, Alvah C. Roebuck. With low prices, free delivery, and a great variety of products, the company grew rapidly. Today, Sears, Roebuck and Company is still one of the most successful retail sales businesses in the world.

Levi Strauss, an immigrant from Germany, left New York City for California in 1850. He made the journey west to sell canvas to settlers to use for sails and for coverings for their wagons. When Strauss arrived there, he found that settlers could not find pants strong enough to last through their hard days working in the gold mines. So Strauss took his canvas material and made it into the first pair of jeans. The company he started became Levi Strauss & Co., the world's largest pants manufacturer.

Sarah Walker was born in 1867 and grew up very poor in rural Louisiana. After moving to St. Louis, Missouri, Walker began selling her homemade beauty products door-to-door. At the time, few companies supplied such products for African American women. Her business, Madame C. J. Walker Manufacturing Company, soon employed more than 3,000 people, most of whom were African American women. Walker was the first woman to become a self-made millionaire in the United States.

Name _____ Date _____

CHART AND GRAPH SKILLS
Read a Double-Bar Graph

Directions Use the double-bar graph to answer the questions.

1 Which Plains state had the highest population in 1900? in 2000?

_____

2 About how many people lived in South Dakota in 1900? in 2000?

_____

_____

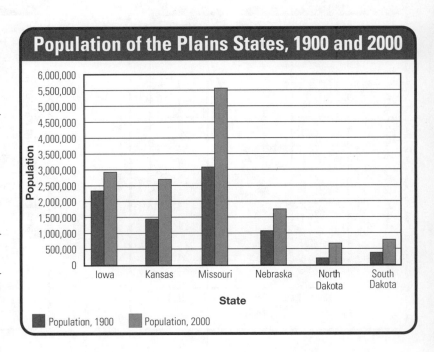

Population of the Plains States, 1900 and 2000

Population (y-axis): 0 to 6,000,000 in increments of 500,000

States (x-axis): Iowa, Kansas, Missouri, Nebraska, North Dakota, South Dakota

■ Population, 1900   ■ Population, 2000

3 How did the population of Nebraska in 1900 compare to its population in 2000?

_____

_____

4 Which state's population changed less between 1900 and 2000, Iowa's or

Kansas's? _____

5 Why do you think North Dakota had the lowest population of the Plains states in

both 1900 and 2000? _____

_____

_____

_____

© Harcourt

Use after reading Chapter 9, Skill Lesson, pages 312–313.

Name _____ Date _____

The Plains States Today

Directions Study the two line graphs below. Then use the information on the graphs to answer the questions that follow.

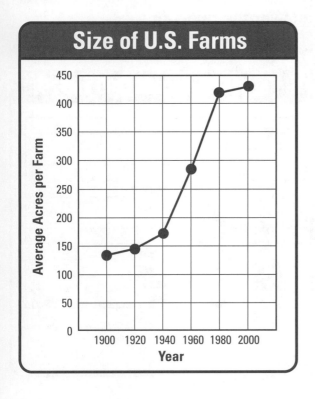

Size of U.S. Farms

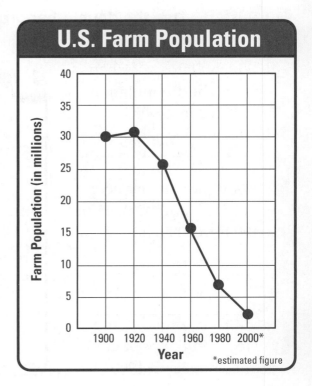

U.S. Farm Population

1. How have farms in the United States changed in the past 100 years?

_____

2. How has the number of people who live on farms in the United States changed in the past 100 years?

_____

3. Which 20-year period shows the biggest increase in the size of farms?

_____

4. About how many fewer people lived on farms in 1960 than in 1900?

_____

Use after reading Chapter 9, Lesson 3, pages 314–319.

© Harcourt

Plains Around the World

Directions Read each statement below. On the line provided, write whether the statement applies to the Pampas of Argentina, the Interior Plains of the United States, or both regions.

INTERIOR PLAINS

EUROPEAN PLAIN

NULLARBOR PLAIN

PAMPAS

1 The western half is much drier than the eastern half. _____

2 It stretches all the way from Canada to Mexico. _____

3 Ranches called *estancias* cover thousands of acres. _____

4 Spanish settlers brought the first cattle and horses. _____

5 It borders the Atlantic Ocean. _____

6 Most early settlers here built sod houses. _____

Directions Read each statement below. On the line provided, write whether the statement applies to the Nullarbor Plain of Australia, the European Plain of Poland, or both regions.

7 Many people here earn a living as farmers. _____

8 Flat land covers most of the region. _____

9 Sheep and cattle ranching are important industries. _____

10 Immigrants from here brought the first winter wheat to the United States. _____

11 It stretches inland from a bay of the Indian Ocean. _____

12 The meaning of its name describes its geography. _____

© Harcourt

Use after reading Chapter 9, Lesson 4, pages 320–323.   **Activity Book** ■ **87**

Plains States

Directions Use this graphic organizer to draw conclusions about the Plains states. To complete it, read each listed fact. Then write any related facts you already know. Finally, draw a conclusion based on your listed facts.

PLAINS STATES

Facts I Know	New Facts	Conclusion
_____ _____ _____ _____	Most early pioneers in the Plains region settled in Missouri or Iowa.	_____ _____ _____ _____
_____ _____ _____ _____	The Plains states are large producers of wheat and corn.	_____ _____ _____ _____
_____ _____ _____ _____	Service industries are the fastest-growing industries in the Plains states today.	_____ _____ _____ _____

Use after reading Chapter 9, pages 294–323.

© Harcourt

Name _____ Date _____

9 Test Preparation

Directions Read each question and choose the best answer. Then fill in the circle for the answer you have chosen. Be sure to fill in the circle completely.

1 During most of their journey to the Plains region, early pioneers traveled over miles of—

   Ⓐ forests.

   Ⓑ wheat fields.

   Ⓒ prairie.

   Ⓓ desert.

2 Which of the following is *not* a way that the Sioux adapted to their new environment on the Great Plains?

   Ⓕ They lived in sod houses instead of log cabins.

   Ⓖ They used horses for travel instead of canoes.

   Ⓗ They hunted buffalo instead of farming the land.

   Ⓙ They burned buffalo chips instead of wood.

3 What is a main difference between the Central Plains and the Great Plains?

   Ⓐ The Central Plains lie farther west than the Great Plains.

   Ⓑ The Central Plains get more precipitation than the Great Plains.

   Ⓒ The Great Plains are more fertile than the Central Plains.

   Ⓓ There are more trees on the Great Plains than on the Central Plains.

4 Which of the following do *not* usually occur in the Plains region?

   Ⓕ blizzards

   Ⓖ tornadoes

   Ⓗ hailstorms

   Ⓙ hurricanes

5 Why is meat packing a large industry in both the Plains region of the United States and the Pampas of Argentina?

   Ⓐ because people in both places eat a lot of meat

   Ⓑ because both places have extensive railroads

   Ⓒ because cattle ranching is a large industry in both places

   Ⓓ because wheat farming is a large industry in both places

© Harcourt

People and Mountains

Exhausted after a hard year of travel, Meriwether Lewis and William Clark finally reached the Rocky Mountains in the late summer of 1805. The Shoshone Indians who lived in the area warned the explorers that crossing those immense mountains would be extremely difficult. Yet Lewis and Clark had to face the challenge in order to reach the Pacific Ocean and complete their journey across North America.

Directions **While crossing the Bitterroot Range of the Rocky Mountains, Lewis and Clark continued to record their adventures in their journals. Read each of their journal entries below. Then draw a picture next to each entry to illustrate the events Lewis and Clark described.**

September 2, 1805

We set out early and proceeded... through thickets [tangled bushes] in which we were obliged to cut a road, over rocky hillsides.... With the greatest of difficulty and risk we made 7 ½ miles.

September 3, 1805

This day we passed over immense hills and some of the worst roads that ever horses passed. Our horses frequently fell. Snow about 2 inches deep when it began to rain and sleet.

(continued)

© Harcourt

Use after reading Chapter 10, Lesson 1, pages 342–347.

Name _____ Date _____

September 15, 1805

Four miles up the mountain. . . .
When we arrived at the top . . .
I could observe high rugged
mountains in every direction as
far as I could see.

September 18, 1805

We marched 18 miles this day
and encamped on the side of a
steep mountain . . . on a bold
running creek, which I call
Hungry Creek, as at that place
we had nothing to eat.

September 19, 1805

The ridge terminated [ended]
and we, to our inexpressible
joy, discovered a large tract
[area] of prairie country lying
to the southwest.

Use after reading Chapter 10, Lesson 1, pages 342–347.

CHART AND GRAPH SKILLS
Read a Cutaway Diagram

Before trains linked the Mountain region to the rest of the country, stagecoaches were the only form of public transportation for travelers heading west. Although journeys by stagecoach were faster than by wagon train, they were long, rough, and uncomfortable. Coaches were usually loaded down with passengers, merchandise, luggage, and mail.

Directions **Study this cutaway diagram of a stagecoach. Then answer the questions that follow.**

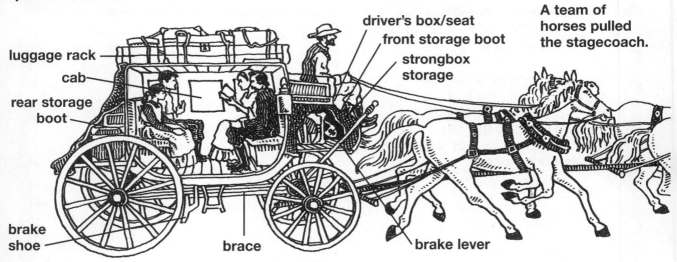

1 What parts of a stagecoach were used for storage?

_____

2 Where did people sit in a stagecoach? _____

_____

3 How did the driver stop the stagecoach? _____

4 Describe some similarities and differences between a stagecoach and a covered

wagon. _____

_____

_____

© Harcourt

Name _____ Date _____

The Mountain States Today

Directions Use the maps on page 94 to answer the questions below.

1 When and where was the first national park established in the United States?

_____

2 Why do the Mountain states have some of the highest elevations in the West?

_____

3 What national park names in the West suggest that they protect mountain areas?

_____

_____

_____

4 What desert regions are located in the West?

_____

_____

5 In what western state were eight national parks established in 1980?

_____

6 What is the elevation of the land along most of the Snake River?

_____

7 What are some of the mountain ranges that make up the Rocky Mountains?

_____

8 What was the first national park established in Utah? When was it established?

_____

_____

(continued)

© Harcourt

Name _____   Date _____

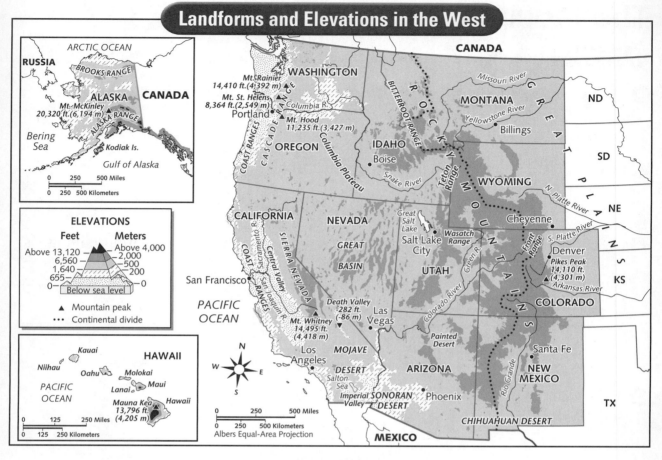

Landforms and Elevations in the West

ARCTIC OCEAN
RUSSIA
BROOKS RANGE
ALASKA   CANADA
Mt. McKinley
20,320 ft.(6,194 m)
ALASKA RANGE
Bering
Sea
Kodiak Is.
Gulf of Alaska
0   250   500 Miles
0   250 500 Kilometers

ELEVATIONS
Feet   Meters
Above 13,120   Above 4,000
6,560   2,000
1,640   500
655   200
0   0
Below sea level
▲ Mountain peak
••• Continental divide

Kauai
Niihau   Oahu   Molokai   HAWAII
Lanai   Maui
PACIFIC
OCEAN   Mauna Kea   Hawaii
13,796 ft.
(4,205 m)
0   125   250 Miles
0   125 250 Kilometers

CANADA
WASHINGTON
Mt. Rainier
14,410 ft.(4,392 m)
Mt. St. Helens
8,364 ft.(2,549 m)
Portland   Columbia R.
Mt. Hood
11,235 ft. (3,427 m)
COAST RANGES   CASCADE RANGE   OREGON   IDAHO   Boise
Columbia Plateau   Snake River
BITTERROOT RANGE   MONTANA   Missouri River
Billings   Yellowstone River   ND
Teton Range   WYOMING   SD
CALIFORNIA   NEVADA   Great Salt Lake   Cheyenne   N. Platte River   NE
GREAT BASIN   Salt Lake City   Wasatch Range   Front Range   S. Platte River   Denver
San Francisco   SIERRA NEVADA   Central Valley   San Joaquin R.   COAST RANGES   UTAH   Green R.   Pikes Peak   14,110 ft. (4,301 m)   KS
PACIFIC OCEAN   Death Valley   -282 ft. (-86 m)   Las Vegas   Colorado River   COLORADO   Arkansas River
Mt. Whitney   14,495 ft. (4,418 m)   Painted Desert   Santa Fe
Los Angeles   MOJAVE DESERT   ARIZONA   NEW MEXICO   Rio Grande
Salton Sea   SONORAN DESERT   Phoenix   TX
Imperial Valley   CHIHUAHUAN DESERT
N
W   E
S
0   250   500 Miles
0   250 500 Kilometers
Albers Equal-Area Projection
MEXICO

National Parks in the West

RUSSIA
Gates of the Arctic (1980)
Kobuk Valley (1980)   AK   CANADA
Lake Clark (1980)   Denali (1980)
Katmai (1980)   Wrangell-St. Elias (1980)
Kenai Fjords (1980)   Glacier Bay (1980)
0   250   500 Miles
0   250 500 Kilometers

PACIFIC
OCEAN

● National park

Haleakala (1960)
HI
Hawai'i Volcanoes (1961)
0   125   250 Miles
0   125 250 Kilometers

North Cascades (1968)
Olympic (1938)   WA
Mount Rainier (1899)
OR
Crater Lake (1902)
Redwood (1968)
Lassen Volcanic (1916)
NV   Great Basin (1986)
CA
Yosemite (1890)
Kings Canyon (1890)
Death Valley (1933)
Sequoia (1890)
Joshua Tree (1936)
Channel Is. (1980)

CANADA
Glacier (1910)
MT   ND   Theodore Roosevelt (1978)   MN   WI
Yellowstone (1872)
ID   SD   Badlands (1939)   IA
Grand Teton (1929)   Wind Cave (1903)
WY   NE   IL
Capitol Reef (1971)   Arches (1971)   Rocky Mountain (1915)
Zion (1919)   UT   CO   KS   MO
Bryce Canyon (1928)   Canyonlands (1964)
Grand Canyon (1919)   AZ   Mesa Verde (1906)   OK   AR
Petrified Forest (1962)
NM
Saguaro (1933)   Carlsbad Caverns (1930)
Guadalupe Mts. (1972)   TX   LA
N
W   E
S
MEXICO
0   125   250 Miles
0   125 250 Kilometers
Albers Equal-Area Projection
Gulf of Mexico

© Harcourt

Use after reading Chapter 10, Lesson 2, pages 350–355.

Name _____ Date _____

Mountains Around the World

Directions Use the following information to complete the tables below.

- The Rocky Mountains extend about 3,750 miles (6,035 km) through North America. The highest peak of the Rockies, Mount Elbert, in Colorado, is 14,433 feet (4,399 m) tall.
- The Himalayas stretch about 1,550 miles (2,494 km) through Asia. At 29,035 feet (8,850 m), Mount Everest is the tallest peak in the Himalayas, as well as the highest point on Earth.
- The Alps run about 660 miles (1,062 km) through southern Europe. Mont Blanc, on the border of France and Italy, is the highest peak in the Alps at 15,771 feet (4,807 m).
- The Atlas Mountains stretch about 1,200 miles (1,931 km) across northern Africa. Mount Toubkal, in Morocco, is the highest peak in the Atlas Mountains. It is 13,671 feet (4,167 m) tall.
- The Andes Mountains are the longest chain of mountains in the world. They run about 5,500 miles (8,851 km) through South America. At 22,834 feet (6,960 m) tall, Mount Aconcagua, in Argentina, is the highest peak in the Andes.

A. To complete Table A, list the mountain ranges in alphabetical order.

B. To complete Table B, list the mountain ranges in order by length from longest to shortest.

C. To complete Table C, list the mountain ranges in order by the height of their tallest peak from highest to lowest.

TABLE A	TABLE B	TABLE C

© Harcourt

Use after reading Chapter 10, Lesson 3, pages 356–361.

Name _____ Date _____

Mountain States

Directions Complete this graphic organizer to make generalizations about mountain regions. Read each set of facts. Then make a generalization based on those facts.

Mountain States

FACT 1	+	FACT 2	→	GENERALIZATION
Pioneers used the wide, flat South Pass to cross the Rockies.	+	Pioneers traveled in covered wagons that mules, horses, or oxen could pull over the mountains.		_____ _____ _____ _____
Farmers in the Mountain states build their farms in the valleys of the Rockies and on the plains and plateaus east and west of the mountains.	+	Quechuan farmers make terraces to grow their crops on the sides of the Andes Mountains.		_____ _____ _____ _____ _____
People mine gold, silver, lead, copper, and coal from the Rocky Mountains.	+	People mine coal, iron, and salt from the Alps. People mine phosphate, iron, copper, lead, natural gas, and zinc from the Atlas Mountains.		_____ _____ _____ _____ _____

Use after reading Chapter 10, pages 340–361.

10 Test Preparation

Directions Read each question and choose the best answer. Then fill in the circle for the answer you have chosen. Be sure to fill in the circle completely.

1 Which river did Lewis and Clark use to reach present-day North Dakota?
   Ⓐ the Mississippi River
   Ⓑ the Missouri River
   Ⓒ the Columbia River
   Ⓓ the Colorado River

2 Which of the following is *not* a way the Rocky Mountains divide North America?
   Ⓕ They affect the flow of many rivers across the continent.
   Ⓖ They separate the Interior Plains from the Intermountain region.
   Ⓗ They form a natural border between the United States and Canada.
   Ⓙ They separate the Middle West region from the West region of the United States.

3 Which of the following is true about most mountain regions?
   Ⓐ They usually have smaller populations than other kinds of regions.
   Ⓑ Agriculture is the most important industry.
   Ⓒ They usually have more large cities than other kinds of regions.
   Ⓓ The climate is always warm and sunny.

4 Which state is the leading coal producer in the United States?
   Ⓕ Colorado
   Ⓖ Montana
   Ⓗ Utah
   Ⓙ Wyoming

5 Which of the following is *not* an animal that lives naturally in high mountain regions?
   Ⓐ a horse
   Ⓑ a llama
   Ⓒ a bighorn sheep
   Ⓓ a yak

The Southwest Desert Long Ago

One place where the Anasazi built settlements was beneath the towering rock walls of Chaco (CHAH•koh) Canyon, in what is today New Mexico.

Directions Use the time line to answer the questions that follow. The *c.* before a date stands for *circa*, which means "around." Historians use the *c.* when they do not know the exact date.

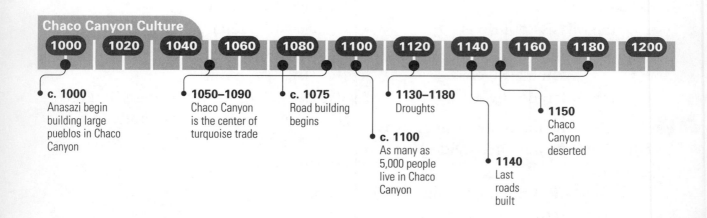

Chaco Canyon Culture

1000 1020 1040 1060 1080 1100 1120 1140 1160 1180 1200

c. 1000
Anasazi begin building large pueblos in Chaco Canyon

1050–1090
Chaco Canyon is the center of turquoise trade

c. 1075
Road building begins

c. 1100
As many as 5,000 people live in Chaco Canyon

1130–1180
Droughts

1140
Last roads built

1150
Chaco Canyon deserted

1 Between what years were Chaco Canyon roads built? _____

_____

2 When did the Anasazi begin building pueblos in Chaco Canyon? _____

_____

3 In what year did as many as 5,000 people live in the Chaco Canyon community?

_____

4 When did the droughts begin in Chaco Canyon? _____

5 How many decades did the droughts last? _____

6 By what year had the Anasazi people left Chaco Canyon? _____

7 About how many years did the Anasazi live in the Chaco Canyon pueblos?

_____

Use after reading Chapter 11, Lesson 1, pages 366–372.

The Southwest Desert States Today

Directions Use the clues below to solve the crossword puzzle on the next page.

Across

1 This is one of the world's largest reservoirs. It holds the waters of the Colorado River. (2 words)

5 The valleys of the Salt River and the _____ _____ were the first parts of the Arizona desert to be settled. (2 words)

6 a deep gully or ditch carved by running water

7 The _____ Desert covers most of southwestern Arizona.

9 a sudden, heavy rain

10 a person who has no permanent home but keeps moving from place to place

11 Most places in the desert receive _____ only a few times a year.

Down

2 someone who moves from farm to farm with the seasons, harvesting crops (2 words)

3 a supply of water that lies deep beneath Earth's surface

4 The _____ Arizona Project was built to help people use less groundwater.

6 a large pipe or canal built to carry water

8 Native Americans of this culture came to the Sonoran Desert about 2,000 years ago.

Directions After completing the crossword puzzle, copy on the lines below the letters that appear in the shaded boxes.

____ ____ ____ ____ ____ ____ ____ ____ ____ ____

Directions Now unscramble the letters above to answer this riddle.

What stands as tall as a 54-story building, contains enough concrete to pave a two-lane highway from New York City to San Francisco, and is shown in the drawing on the next page (2 words)?

____ ____ ____ ____ ____ ____ ____ ____ ____ ____

(continued)

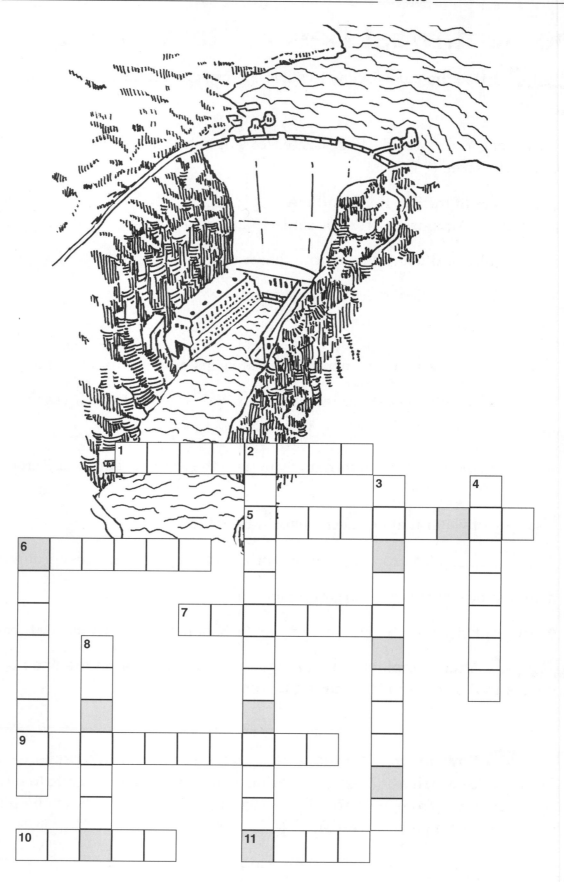

Name _____ Date _____

READING SKILLS

Predict a Likely Outcome

The following statements provide information about conditions in Grand Canyon National Park.

- More than 5 million people visit the Grand Canyon each year.
- Almost 2 million cars and more than 30,000 tour buses drive into the park each year.
- Glen Canyon Dam changes the amount of water flowing in the Colorado River through the Grand Canyon.
- Many roads, trails, and buildings in the park badly need repairs, which would cost millions of dollars.

Directions Use the information above to make predictions about Grand Canyon National Park.

1 **Look at the information you already have about the topic.**
How have humans changed Grand Canyon National Park?

_____

2 **Gather any other information that relates to the topic.**
What do you already know about the Grand Canyon?

_____

_____

3 **Look for patterns in these events or data.**
How do you think human actions are affecting Grand Canyon National Park?

_____

_____

4 **Make a prediction based on any patterns you discover and your own experiences.**
What do you think Grand Canyon National Park might be like in the future?

_____

_____

Deserts of the World

To most people who do not live in desert regions, water seems to be a plentiful resource. However, less than 1 gallon (about 4 L) out of every 100 gallons (379 L) of water on Earth is fresh water that people can use. People all over the world are using enormous amounts of water every day to drink, cook, wash, grow food, and manufacture products. Which parts of the world have enough water and which parts do not? How do people around the world use their water resources?

Directions **Use the map and the graph on page 103 to answer these questions.**

1 Which parts of North America have the least amount of available water per person?

_____

2 How is most of Earth's fresh water used?

_____

3 Which part of Asia has the most amount of available water per person?

_____

4 On which continent do people use the most water? the least?

_____

5 Where on Earth do people use more water for industry than for agriculture?

_____

6 Which continent has more available water per person, Africa or Australia?

_____

7 Look at the map on page 382 in your textbook. How does the information on that map relate to the information on the map on page 103?

_____

_____

_____

(continued)

Use after reading Chapter 11, Lesson 3, pages 381–385.

© Harcourt

Name _____ Date _____

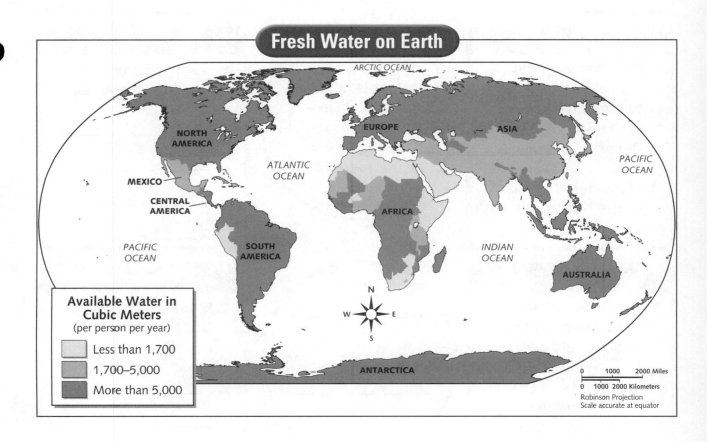

World Water Usage

Amount per Person per Year (in cubic meters)

1,300
1,200
1,100
1,000
900
800
700
600
500
400
300
200
100
0

North America   Oceania (Australia and Pacific Islands)   Europe   Asia   South America   Africa

World Region

■ Agriculture   ■ Industy   ■ Domestic

Fresh Water on Earth

ARCTIC OCEAN

NORTH AMERICA   EUROPE   ASIA

ATLANTIC OCEAN   PACIFIC OCEAN

MEXICO

CENTRAL AMERICA   AFRICA

PACIFIC OCEAN   SOUTH AMERICA   INDIAN OCEAN

AUSTRALIA

Available Water in Cubic Meters
(per person per year)

☐ Less than 1,700
☐ 1,700–5,000
■ More than 5,000

ANTARCTICA

N
W   E
S

0   1000   2000 Miles
0   1000 2000 Kilometers
Robinson Projection
Scale accurate at equator

Southwest Desert States

Directions Complete the following graphic organizer to make inferences about some of the main ideas in the chapter. Read the information that is given. Then fill in the missing statements.

SOUTHWEST DESERT STATES

Facts

1. Early peoples in the Southwest Desert region were farmers.

2. They used materials they found around them to build their homes.

Inference

_____
_____
_____
_____

Your Experiences

1. Growing food requires water.

2. Few trees grow in the desert.

Facts

1. People have built _____ across rivers to create reservoirs in the Southwest Desert states.

2. Many people land-scape their yards with _____ .

Inference

People in the Southwest Desert states try to manage their water resources carefully.

Your Experiences

1. Reservoirs are one way to store water.

2. _____
_____
_____
_____

Facts

1. The Atacama and Gobi Deserts have cool or cold climates.

2. Most parts of the Sahara and the Negev get less than 5 inches (13 cm) of rain each year.

Inference

_____
_____
_____
_____

Your Experiences

1. Most deserts in the United States have hot climates.

2. _____
_____
_____
_____

Use after reading Chapter 11, pages 364–385.

11 Test Preparation

Name _____ Date _____

Directions Read each question and choose the best answer. Then fill in the circle for the answer you have chosen. Be sure to fill in the circle completely.

1 Through what desert did Coronado travel while exploring the Southwest Desert region?
  Ⓐ the Sonoran Desert
  Ⓑ the Chihuahuan Desert
  Ⓒ the Great Basin
  Ⓓ the Painted Desert

2 Why did the Anasazi Indians build their homes with adobe?
  Ⓕ because adobe walls were thin
  Ⓖ because few trees grew in the Four Corners' dry climate
  Ⓗ because the tall adobe buildings provided shade for their crops
  Ⓙ because the Anasazi Indians were nomads

3 Which of the following is *not* a natural source of fresh water in deserts?
  Ⓐ cloudbursts
  Ⓑ oases
  Ⓒ reservoirs
  Ⓓ snow

4 Which of the following is *not* a reason why the population of the Southwest Desert states is growing rapidly?
  Ⓕ People have created new sources of water in the region.
  Ⓖ The region has a generally sunny, warm climate.
  Ⓗ People have created a steady supply of electricity in the region.
  Ⓙ Millions of acres in the region are set aside as national parks and forests.

5 Which desert region has a generally cool climate?
  Ⓐ the Atacama Desert
  Ⓑ the Negev
  Ⓒ the North American Desert
  Ⓓ the Sahara

Heading to the Pacific

Directions Changes in technology have reduced the amount of time needed to travel from coast to coast in the United States. Use the table below to answer the questions that follow about traveling west over the years.

Travel Time from Coast to Coast

YEAR	METHOD	TIME
1840	By Wagon	6 Months
1850	By Clipper Ship	3–4 Months
1861	By Train and Stagecoach	26 Days
1869	By Train	7 Days
1932	By Airplane	24 Hours
2000	By Jet	5 Hours

San Francisco

New York City

1 What methods of transportation could forty-niners use to reach California during the gold rush? How long did each trip take?

_____

2 How much time did it take travelers to go from coast to coast in 1861? How much time did they save after the transcontinental railroad was completed?

_____

3 How much less time does a jet flight across the country take today than an

airplane flight did 70 years ago? _____

4 If you were planning to travel from New York City to San Francisco in 1900, which of the transportation methods in the chart would you prefer to use? Why?

_____

Use after reading Chapter 12, Lesson 1, pages 390–395.

MAP AND GLOBE SKILLS
Use a Time Zone Map

Directions Use the time zone map below to answer the questions on page 108.

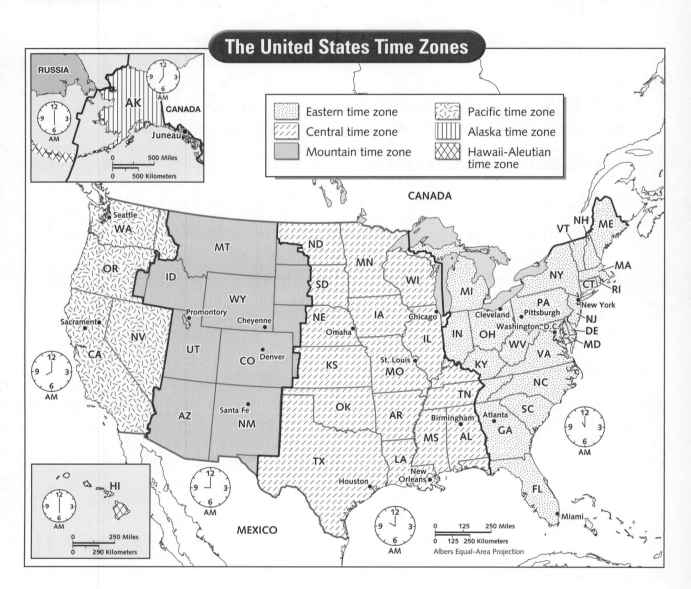

The United States Time Zones

Eastern time zone
Central time zone
Mountain time zone
Pacific time zone
Alaska time zone
Hawaii-Aleutian time zone

(continued)

© Harcourt

Name _____ Date _____

1 In which time zone do you live? _____

2 When it is 4:00 P.M. in New Mexico, what time is it in

    a. Maine? _____   **d.** California? _____

    b. Hawaii? _____   **e.** Colorado? _____

    c. Minnesota? _____   **f.** Georgia? _____

3 The Union Pacific Railroad built west from Omaha, Nebraska. The Central Pacific Railroad built east from Sacramento, California. The two railroads met at Promontory, Utah, in 1869 to complete the transcontinental railroad.

    a. If it is 7:00 P.M. in Sacramento, what time is it in Omaha? _____

    b. If it is 8:00 A.M. in Omaha, what time is it in Sacramento? _____

    c. If it is 10:00 A.M. in Promontory, what time is it in Omaha? in Sacramento?

_____

4 Many offices open at 9:00 A.M. and close at 5:00 P.M. If you live in Nevada and you want to call an office in New York, when is the earliest time you could call?

the latest time? _____

5 Some states are in two different time zones. That means that people in neighboring towns might set their clocks differently! Study the map. Then list five states

that have more than one time zone. _____

_____

_____

6 It is noon in St. Louis, Missouri. Draw hands on the clocks below, showing the correct time for each city.

SEATTLE   **PITTSBURGH**   **JUNEAU**   **DENVER**

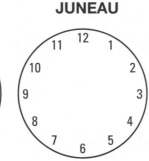

© Harcourt

Land and Climate in the Pacific States

Directions The tables below show average monthly temperatures (in degrees Fahrenheit) and precipitation levels (in inches) for three cities in the Pacific states. Use this information to answer the questions that follow.

ANCHORAGE, ALASKA												
	JAN	FEB	MAR	APRIL	MAY	JUNE	JULY	AUG	SEPT	OCT	NOV	DEC
Temperature	15	19	26	36	47	54	58	56	48	35	21	18
Precipitation	0.8	0.8	0.7	0.7	0.7	1.1	1.7	2.4	2.7	2.0	1.1	1.1

SAN DIEGO, CALIFORNIA												
	JAN	FEB	MAR	APRIL	MAY	JUNE	JULY	AUG	SEPT	OCT	NOV	DEC
Temperature	57	59	60	62	64	67	71	73	71	68	62	57
Precipitation	1.8	1.5	1.8	0.8	0.2	0.1	0	0.1	0.2	0.4	1.5	1.6

SEATTLE, WASHINGTON												
	JAN	FEB	MAR	APRIL	MAY	JUNE	JULY	AUG	SEPT	OCT	NOV	DEC
Temperature	41	44	47	50	56	61	65	66	61	54	46	42
Precipitation	5.4	4.0	3.8	2.5	1.8	1.6	0.9	1.2	1.9	3.3	5.7	6.0

1 Which city is the warmest in December? _____

2 Which city is the coolest in July? _____

3 Which city has the driest climate? the wettest climate? _____

_____

4 How do the locations of Anchorage, Alaska, and San Diego, California, help explain the similarities and differences in their climates?

_____

_____

5 Based on climate, in which of these three Pacific cities would you like to live? Explain your answer on a separate sheet of paper.

Living in the Pacific States

Directions Each of the following viewpoints was expressed in "A River Dammed," a recent *National Geographic* article about dams built across the Columbia River system. Read the viewpoints. Then answer the questions.

Viewpoint A

"We have taken the Columbia River system beyond the point of balance, and the question now is, do you undo some of this development?"—Michele DeHart

Viewpoint B

"In the old days, we were at the whim of nature here. If we didn't have the rainfall, we couldn't grow our crops. And then we got the water from the dams, and it changed everything."—Bill Watson

Viewpoint C

"Nobody ever said that salmon and dams were made for each other. People needed power. It was a public policy choice."—Dutch Meier

Viewpoint D

"From a biological standpoint, the only way to recover the salmon with any high likelihood of success is to breach [break open] the dams."—Ed Bowles

Viewpoint E

"Fishing is not just a buck for us. It's a way of life. This is a very important part of our culture. . . . And that's all been taken away from us."—Steve Fick

From "Straight Talk" by Rachel Buchholtz in *National Geographic WORLD* Magazine, January/February 2002. Text copyright © 2001 by National Geographic Society. Reprinted by permission of National Geographic Society, 1145 17th Street, N. W., Washington, DC 20036.

1 Which viewpoints contain opinions in favor of the dams? _____

2 Which viewpoints contain opinions against the dams? _____

3 Match each of the people below with the viewpoint he or she expressed above:

a biologist _____

a potato farmer _____

a fisher _____

a government leader _____

an environmentalist _____

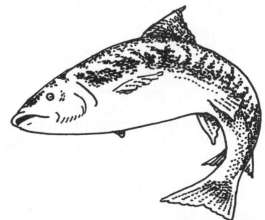

Name _____ Date _____

CITIZENSHIP SKILLS
Act as a Responsible Citizen

Directions One way to act as a responsible citizen is to write a letter to an elected official about an issue that concerns you. First, identify an issue or a problem in your community that interests you. Then, on a separate sheet of paper, use the format below to write a letter describing the issue or problem to a community leader.

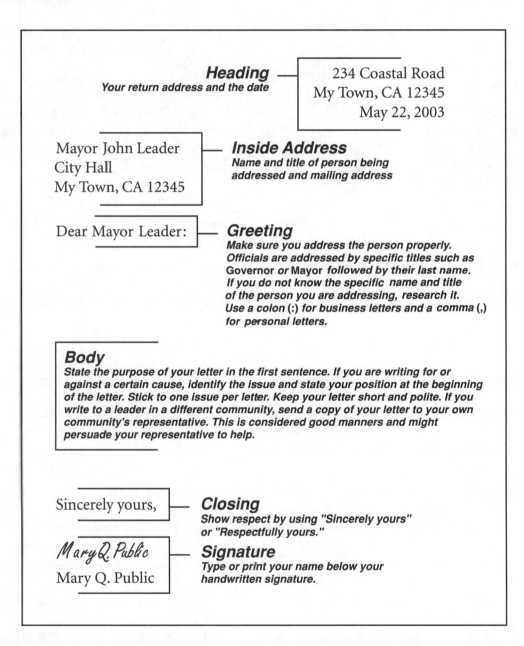

Heading —— 234 Coastal Road
Your return address and the date My Town, CA 12345
May 22, 2003

Mayor John Leader
City Hall
My Town, CA 12345

Inside Address
Name and title of person being addressed and mailing address

Dear Mayor Leader: —— **Greeting**
Make sure you address the person properly. Officials are addressed by specific titles such as Governor or Mayor followed by their last name. If you do not know the specific name and title of the person you are addressing, research it. Use a colon (:) for business letters and a comma (,) for personal letters.

Body
State the purpose of your letter in the first sentence. If you are writing for or against a certain cause, identify the issue and state your position at the beginning of the letter. Stick to one issue per letter. Keep your letter short and polite. If you write to a leader in a different community, send a copy of your letter to your own community's representative. This is considered good manners and might persuade your representative to help.

Sincerely yours, —— **Closing**
Show respect by using "Sincerely yours" or "Respectfully yours."

Mary Q. Public —— **Signature**
Mary Q. Public *Type or print your name below your handwritten signature.*

Name _____   Date _____

Americans in the Pacific

Directions The seal of a state often contains symbols that tell about the geography, history, and heritage of that state. Study the state seal of Hawaii and the captions that explain it. Then answer the questions that follow.

Pacific sunset

King Kamehameha I, who united the Hawaiian Islands in the 1700s

The phoenix, a legendary bird that rises from the ashes of a fire

The state motto: Hawaiian for "The life of the land is perpetuated [made to last a long time] in righteousness [justice]"

The year Hawaii became a state

The shield of Hawaii's royal family

Lady Liberty carrying Hawaii's state flag

Taro and banana leaves and maiden-hair ferns, typical Hawaiian plants

1 When did Hawaii become a state? _____

2 Which parts of the state seal show that Hawaii was once ruled by monarchs?

_____

3 Why do you think the seal includes a sunset? _____

_____

4 Why do you think the seal shows a legendary bird rising from fire?

_____

5 What items might you include if you were designing a new state seal for your

state? _____

_____

Directions On a separate sheet of paper, create a personal seal. Use drawings that tell about your personal history and things that you like to do. Make sure you include your name and a personal motto (some words to live by).

Use after reading Chapter 12, Lesson 4, pages 412–415.

© Harcourt

Oceans Around the World

In 1519 a Portuguese explorer named Ferdinand Magellan sailed from his homeland in search of a water route to Asia. The members of this expedition became the first people to sail around the world.

Directions The map below shows the route that Magellan's ships followed around the world. Use the map to answer the questions that follow.

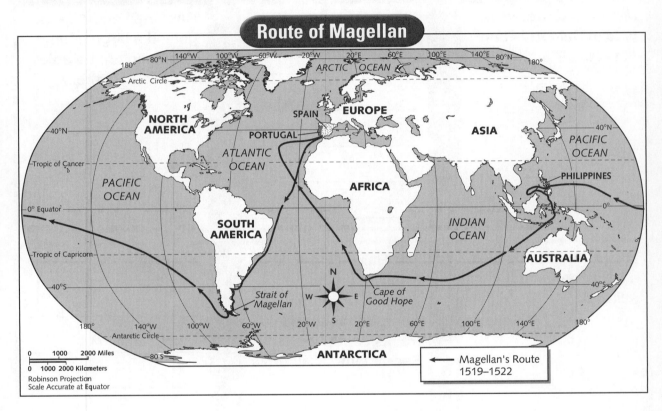

Route of Magellan

1. Where did Magellan begin his voyage? _____

2. In which direction did the expedition set sail? _____

3. At what point did Magellan's ships enter the Pacific Ocean? _____

   _____

4. What group of Pacific islands did the ships visit? _____

5. List in order the oceans Magellan's ships sailed. What is the only ocean they did

   not reach? _____

   _____

   _____

Name _____ Date _____

Pacific States

Directions Complete this graphic organizer to predict outcomes of some events that occurred in the Pacific states.

PACIFIC STATES

EVENT	FACTS	OUTCOME
Miners discovered gold in California and Alaska.	_____ _____ _____ _____ _____ _____	California and Alaska gained a large enough population to be able to become states.
The United States built a transcontinental railroad.	The Union Pacific laid tracks west from Omaha, Nebraska. The Central Pacific laid tracks east from Sacramento, California.	_____ _____ _____ _____ _____
People built dams across rivers in the Pacific states.	_____ _____ _____ _____ _____	_____ _____ _____ _____ _____

Use after reading Chapter 12, pages 388–419.

Name _____ Date _____

12 Test Preparation

Directions Read each question and choose the best answer. Then fill in the circle for the answer you have chosen. Be sure to fill in the circle completely.

1 Between which two mountain ranges does the Willamette Valley lie?
- Ⓐ the Cascade Range and the Sierra Nevada
- Ⓑ the Sierra Nevada and the Coast Ranges
- Ⓒ the Rocky Mountains and the Sierra Nevada
- Ⓓ the Cascade Range and the Coast Ranges

2 In which Pacific state was gold *not* discovered?
- Ⓕ Alaska
- Ⓖ California
- Ⓗ Hawaii
- Ⓙ Washington

3 An earthquake is caused by—
- Ⓐ strong winds and high waves hitting the Pacific coastline.
- Ⓑ the movement and cracking of layers of rock deep inside Earth.
- Ⓒ the rain shadow created by the western mountains.
- Ⓓ an opening in Earth's surface out of which hot gases, ash, and lava pour.

4 Which of the following is *not* a major industry in the Pacific Northwest?
- Ⓕ lumber production
- Ⓖ fishing for salmon and tuna
- Ⓗ drilling for oil and natural gas
- Ⓙ airplane manufacturing

5 Which is the world's largest ocean?
- Ⓐ the Arctic Ocean
- Ⓑ the Atlantic Ocean
- Ⓒ the Indian Ocean
- Ⓓ the Pacific Ocean

Name _____ Date _____

Many Places, People, and Ways

Directions Use the information in the table and bar graph below to answer the questions that follow.

People in the United States, 2000	
Ancestry	**Population**
African American	31,606,957
Asian American	10,313,119
European American	190,433,375
Hispanic American	34,334,480
Native American and Native Alaskan American	1,823,395
Native Hawaiian and Pacific Islander American	380,706

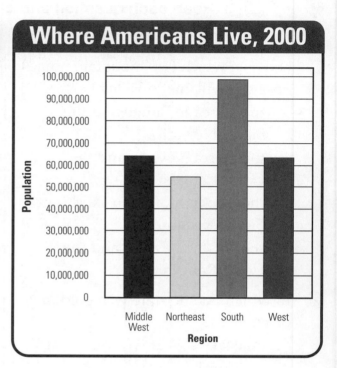

Where Americans Live, 2000

1 What is the ancestry of the largest group of people in the United States?

_____

2 In which region of the United States do the most people live? _____

3 How many Asian Americans live in the United States? _____

4 About how many people live in the Northeast region of the United States?

_____

5 Which two ethnic groups in the United States have about the same number

of people? _____

6 Which two regions in the United States have about the same number of people?

_____

Use after reading Chapter 13, Lesson 1, pages 438–443.

Name _____ Date _____

MAP AND GLOBE SKILLS

Read a Population Map

Directions The size of each state shown on the map below is based on the total population of the state, not on its area, or geographic size. Examine this map, and then compare it with the maps of the United States on pages 428–429 and page 445 in your textbook. Then answer the questions on page 118.

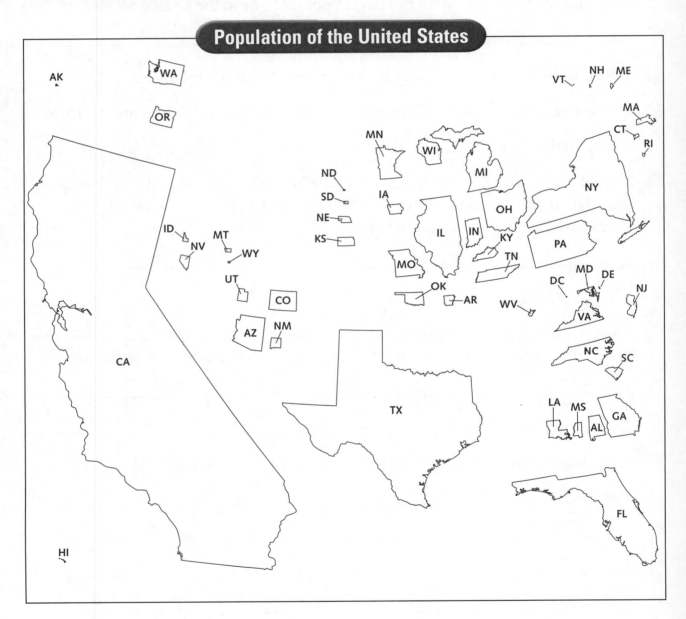

Population of the United States

(continued)

© Harcourt

1 Alaska is the largest state in geographic terms in the United States. Why is it one of the smallest states on the map on page 117?

_____

2 Why does the map on page 117 show California as the largest state?

_____

3 What are the five states with the largest populations in the United States?

_____

4 Which state has a larger population—Pennsylvania or Oregon? _____

5 Of the three states Arkansas, Georgia, and Mississippi, which two are the closest

in population? _____

6 Find North Dakota and South Dakota on the map on page 117 and on the map on page 428 in your textbook. What general statement can you make about those states based on their sizes on each map?

_____

_____

7 The population of New Mexico is almost 2 million. About how many people live in Oregon? How did you use the map on page 117 to answer this question?

_____

_____

8 How does the map on page 117 compare with the map on page 445 in your

textbook? _____

_____

_____

_____

Use after reading Chapter 13, Skill Lesson, pages 444–445.

A United Country

During the War of 1812, Francis Scott Key stood on the deck of a ship, watching the British fire rockets and bombs at Fort McHenry, which guarded Baltimore, Maryland. At dawn the next day, the American flag still flew over the fort. Key wrote a poem describing the battle and his patriotic feelings. Key's poem was set to music and became very popular. In 1931 the United States government officially declared Key's song the national anthem. It has helped unite Americans ever since.

Directions **Read the first verse of "The Star-Spangled Banner" below. Then follow the instructions at the bottom of the page.**

Oh, say can you see by the dawn's early light
What so proudly we hail'd at the twilight's last gleaming,
Whose broad stripes and bright stars through the perilous fight
O'er the ramparts we watch'd were so gallantly streaming?
And the rockets' red glare, the bombs bursting in air,
Gave proof through the night that our flag was still there.
Oh, say does that star-spangled banner yet wave
O'er the land of the free and the home of the brave?

1. Many countries' national anthems celebrate battles and struggles. Underline the words in the first verse of "The Star-Spangled Banner" that describe the Battle of Fort McHenry.

2. The "banner" in the song is the American flag. Circle the words in the verse that describe the American flag.

3. Two words in this verse describe the people of the United States. Find these two words and underline them twice.

4. On a separate sheet of paper, write a short poem or a verse to a song about an experience that has made you feel proud to be an American.

© Harcourt

Name _____ Date _____

READING SKILLS

Determine Points of View

Directions Read the following statements that some American students recently made about the many different cultures in the United States. Then, on the lines below, describe the points of view you think the students were expressing.

"Some people think that everyone needs to be like them, and that anyone who's different is bad. That's just because those people don't know anything about other cultures."
—Lili, age 10

"In the United States so many people come from so many places that it's really important for every-one to cooperate."
—Aliyeh, age 12

"People are sometimes scared of others who are different from them. But once they get to know them they find out they're not scary—just different."
—Nicholas, age 10

"If someone from a certain culture is not acting very nice, understand that not everyone from that culture acts that way. We shouldn't judge a whole culture by one person. If you are a good person, you are a good person."
—Zaki, age 12

"If people would understand that we're all the same inside, then maybe our differences wouldn't seem so big."
—Ashley, age 12

"One girl at my school was from another country. A lot of people made fun of her because of the way she looked and talked, but I made friends with her. When you get to know people better, you respect them more."
—Maryam, age 11

_____

_____

_____

_____

Directions On a separate sheet of paper, write a statement to express your point of view about the many different cultures in the United States.

Use after reading Chapter 13, Skill Lesson, pages 452–453.

Name _____ Date _____

The United States Economy

People often do work based on the kinds of resources available in their region. The table on the right lists some of the resources, products, or industries of several states. The "Jobs Offered" chart on the left lists different jobs in the United States.

Directions Match each job with the state where it is likely to be offered. Write the letter of the correct state in the box to the left of each job.

Jobs Offered	
	1. Fisher
	2. Miner
	3. Subway car designer
	4. Paper mill worker
	5. Cheese maker
	6. Denim factory worker
	7. Computer programmer
	8. Bread maker
	9. Fruit juice packager
	10. Oil pipeline builder

State Information	
State	Some Resources, Products, or Industries
a. Alaska	Oil, natural gas
b. Florida	Orange and grapefruit groves
c. Maine	Timber, forestry, pulp
d. Ohio	Transportation equipment, farm machinery
e. North Dakota	Wheat farming
f. South Carolina	Cotton farming
g. Texas	High-tech and aerospace industries
h. Washington	Rivers, ocean ports, fishing
i. West Virginia	Coal, gravel, crushed stone
j. Wisconsin	Dairy farming

© Harcourt

Name _____   Date _____

CITIZENSHIP SKILLS
Make Economic Choices

Directions Imagine that you have $20 to spend. Complete the graphic organizer below to help you make an economic choice.

CHOICES
List three $20 items you would like to buy.

⬇   ⬇   ⬇

⬇   ⬇   ⬇

OPPORTUNITY COSTS
List the value that each item has to you.

⬇   ⬇   ⬇

⬇   ⬇   ⬇

ECONOMIC CHOICES

Compare the value of what you will be giving up, or the opportunity cost, for each choice. What are you willing to give up, or trade off? Make an economic choice based on which item will best meet your needs with the $20 you have to spend. List that item below. Your other choices become your opportunity costs.

_____

Use after reading Chapter 13, Skill Lesson, pages 460–461.

Name _____ Date _____

We the People

Directions Complete this graphic organizer to show that you understand the causes and effects of some important facts about the United States today.

WE THE PEOPLE

CAUSE		EFFECT

| People have come from all over the world to live in the United States. |  | _____ _____ _____ |

| _____ _____ _____ |  | The Sun Belt is one of the fastest-growing regions in the United States. |

| The United States government is a democracy. |  | _____ _____ _____ |

| _____ _____ _____ |  | Americans share a way of life. |

| The United States has a free enterprise economy. | | _____ _____ _____ |

13 Test Preparation

Directions Read each question and choose the best answer. Then fill in the circle for the answer you have chosen. Be sure to fill in the circle completely.

1 From where do most immigrants to the United States now come?

- Ⓐ Europe
- Ⓑ Australia
- Ⓒ South America
- Ⓓ Latin America

2 Patriotism is—

- Ⓕ love of one's country.
- Ⓖ a saying chosen to express the ideals of a group.
- Ⓗ an unfair feeling of hatred or dislike for a group.
- Ⓙ something that is built to remind people of the past.

3 Which of the following is *not* a right that all citizens of the United States have?

- Ⓐ the right to say what they think about the government
- Ⓑ the right to never pay taxes
- Ⓒ the right to worship as they please
- Ⓓ the right to have a fair trial

4 What is the goal of nearly every business?

- Ⓕ to loan and borrow money
- Ⓖ to buy goods and sell them directly to consumers
- Ⓗ to make a profit
- Ⓙ to organize, share, and use information

5 The United States takes part in the global economy by—

- Ⓐ trading goods and services with different countries.
- Ⓑ producing computers and using the Internet.
- Ⓒ buying large amounts of goods from producers and selling them to other businesses.
- Ⓓ studying and managing its methods of production.

A Plan of Government

The Constitution of the United States begins with the Preamble, or introduction. The Preamble tells why the Constitution was written. It explains that the writers wanted to set up a fair form of government and make sure of certain freedoms—for themselves and for future American citizens.

Directions **Read the Preamble of the United States Constitution below. Then figure out what the numbered lines mean. Write each number next to the line's best explanation.**

We the people of the United States,
in order to form a more perfect Union,[1]
establish justice,
insure domestic tranquility,[2]
provide for the common defense,
promote the general welfare,[3]
and secure the blessings of liberty
to ourselves and our posterity,[4]
do ordain and establish[5]
this Constitution for the United States of America.

A. _____ make sure there is peace at home

B. _____ to everyone belonging to this country and all who later become part of this country

C. _____ make official and set up

D. _____ encourage health, happiness, and comfort

E. _____ to make a better, single government

© Harcourt

CHART AND GRAPH SKILLS
Read a Flow Chart

Directions The flow chart below shows some of the powers of each branch
of the federal government and how the system of checks and balances applies
to each branch. Use the flow chart to answer the questions that follow.

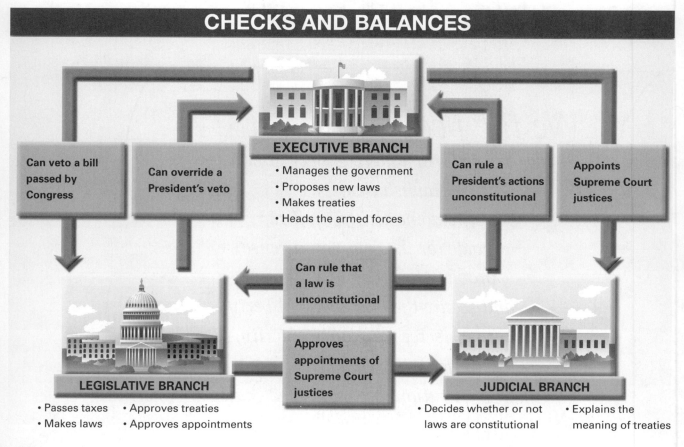

CHECKS AND BALANCES

EXECUTIVE BRANCH
• Manages the government
• Proposes new laws
• Makes treaties
• Heads the armed forces

Can veto a bill passed by Congress

Can override a President's veto

Can rule a President's actions unconstitutional

Appoints Supreme Court justices

Can rule that a law is unconstitutional

Approves appointments of Supreme Court justices

LEGISLATIVE BRANCH
• Passes taxes   • Approves treaties
• Makes laws   • Approves appointments

JUDICIAL BRANCH
• Decides whether or not   • Explains the
  laws are constitutional   meaning of treaties

1 According to the flow chart, how does each branch of the federal government

affect laws in the United States? _____

_____

_____

2 How are vetoes an important part of the checks and balances system in the

federal government? _____

_____

_____

Levels of Government

Directions Complete the three charts below by filling in the correct information for each level of government in the United States. Describe each branch in each level of government, each level's main job, and some of the services each level provides. If you need help, reread Chapter 14, Lesson 2, in your textbook.

FEDERAL GOVERNMENT	
Executive Branch	
Legislative Branch	
Judicial Branch	
Main Job	
Some Services It Provides	

STATE GOVERNMENTS	
Executive Branch	
Legislative Branch	
Judicial Branch	
Main Job	
Some Services They Provide	

LOCAL GOVERNMENTS	
Executive Branch	
Legislative Branch	
Judicial Branch	
Main Job	
Some Services They Provide	

© Harcourt

Name _____ Date _____

United States Citizenship

Directions The declaration below was written in 1913 by the National Child Labor Committee, an organization that worked to outlaw child labor. At that time thousands of young people in the United States did not go to school. Instead, they worked long hours both day and night in factories, mines, and other industries. Read the declaration. Then answer the questions on page 129.

Declaration of Dependency by the Children of America in Mines and Factories and Workshops Assembled

WHEREAS, We, Children of America, are declared to have been born free and equal, and

WHEREAS, We are yet in bondage [slavery] in this land of the free; are forced to toil the long day or the long night, with no control over the conditions of labor, as to health or safety or hours or wages, and with no right to the rewards of our service, therefore be it

RESOLVED, I—That childhood is endowed with [granted] certain inherent [natural] and inalienable rights, among which are freedom from toil for daily bread; the right to play and to dream; the right to the normal sleep of the night season; the right to an education, that we may have equality of opportunity for developing all that there is in us of mind and heart.

RESOLVED, II—That we declare ourselves to be helpless and dependent; that we are and of right ought to be dependent, and that we hereby present the appeal of our helplessness that we may be protected in the enjoyment of the rights of childhood.

RESOLVED, III—That we demand the restoration of our rights by the abolition [ending] of child labor in America.

Alexander J. McKelway, 1913

(continued)

Use after reading Chapter 14, Lesson 3, pages 482–487.

Name _____ Date _____

1 For whom did the National Child Labor Committee claim to speak?

_____

2 What demand does the declaration make?

_____

3 According to the declaration, what hardships did child workers face during the early 1900s in the United States?

_____

_____

_____

4 According to the declaration, with what rights are all children born?

_____

_____

_____

Directions Complete the chart below by listing five rights that you think all young people in the United States should have. For each right, describe why you feel that right is important and what you think your responsibility is concerning that right.

RIGHTS OF YOUNG AMERICANS	
What do you think is your right?	Why is each right important? What is your responsibility?
1.	
2.	
3.	
4.	
5.	

The United States and the World

After World War II ended in 1945, the United States government started a program to involve private citizens in world affairs. By helping individuals around the world form personal relationships, the government hoped to lessen the chance of future world conflicts. Today the program the government started is called Sister Cities International. It helps communities in the United States form special partnerships with communities around the world to increase global cooperation and understanding.

Directions The table below lists the largest city in each of the four major regions of the United States and some of their sister cities. Find the city located in the region where you live, and choose one of its sister cities that you think is interesting. Then, on a separate sheet of paper, write a letter to a fourth grader living in that sister city. Explain the location of your city relative to the sister city's. Describe your region's geography, economy, and history. Share what you like about living where you do and tell about things you do for fun. Finally, explain how you think writing a personal letter like this can help form good relations among people and countries around the world.

UNITED STATES CITY	SISTER CITIES AROUND THE WORLD
Chicago, Illinois	Moscow, Russia; Paris, France; Toronto, Canada
Houston, Texas	Istanbul, Turkey; Perth, Australia; Shenzhen, China
Los Angeles, California	Athens, Greece; Berlin, Germany; Mexico City, Mexico
New York City, New York	Cairo, Egypt; Rome, Italy; Tokyo, Japan

© Harcourt

Name _____ Date _____

Our Country's Government

Directions Complete this graphic organizer by describing different points of view expressed in this chapter.

OUR COUNTRY'S GOVERNMENT

GOVERNMENT

"Governments are instituted among Men, deriving their just Powers from the Consent of the Governed." —President Thomas Jefferson	Details	Point of View
	_____	_____
	_____	_____
	_____	_____
	_____	_____
	_____	_____

CIVIL RIGHTS

"I have a dream that my four little children will one day live in a nation where they will not be judged by the color of their skin, but by the content of their character." —Dr. Martin Luther King, Jr.	Details	Point of View
	_____	_____
	_____	_____
	_____	_____
	_____	_____
	_____	_____

WORLD AFFAIRS

"Observe good faith and justice toward all nations. Cultivate peace and harmony with all." —President George Washington	Details	Point of View
	_____	_____
	_____	_____
	_____	_____
	_____	_____
	_____	_____

© Harcourt

Use after reading Chapter 14, pages 464–491.

Name _____   Date _____

14 Test Preparation

Directions Read each question and choose the best answer. Then fill in the circle for the answer you have chosen. Be sure to fill in the circle completely.

1 What document explains how our federal government works?
- Ⓐ the Declaration of Independence
- Ⓑ the Constitution of the United States
- Ⓒ the Emancipation Proclamation
- Ⓓ the Bill of Rights

2 Who makes sure that laws in the United States are applied fairly?
- Ⓕ the Supreme Court
- Ⓖ the House of Representatives
- Ⓗ the Senate
- Ⓙ the President of the United States

3 Which level of government prints and coins money in the United States?
- Ⓐ the federal government
- Ⓑ the state governments
- Ⓒ the county governments
- Ⓓ the city governments

4 The Civil Rights movement worked to—
- Ⓕ reduce taxes and balance the national budget.
- Ⓖ ensure the rights of citizens to equal treatment under the law.
- Ⓗ provide money, goods, and services for countries in need.
- Ⓙ form alliances to solve international problems.

5 Why does the United States often provide foreign aid?
- Ⓐ to fund international scientific projects
- Ⓑ to protect Earth's environment
- Ⓒ to help countries reach peaceful agreements to conflicts
- Ⓓ to address the world's problems of poverty, hunger, and disease

© Harcourt

Use after reading Chapter 14, pages 464–491.